S0-CCN-876

"I will sing to Jehovah throughout my life;
I will make melody to my God as long as I am."

—PSALM 104:33

NAME _____

CONGREGATION _____

© 2009
WATCH TOWER BIBLE AND TRACT SOCIETY OF PENNSYLVANIA
All Rights Reserved

Publishers
WATCHTOWER BIBLE AND TRACT SOCIETY OF NEW YORK, INC.
Brooklyn, New York, U.S.A.

2010 Printing

This publication is not for sale. It is provided as part of a worldwide
Bible educational work supported by voluntary donations.

Sing to Jehovah
English (*sn*-E)

Made in the United States of America

Sing to Jehovah

1 Jehovah's Attributes

(Revelation 4:11)

Je - ho - vah God, ex - alt - ed in might,
Your loft - y throne, on jus - tice it stands.
Great - est of all is your per - fect love.

Source of all life and Pro - vid - er of light. Cre -
Thus you make known all your righ - teous com - mands. And
None can re - pay all your gifts from a - bove. Your

a - tion speaks of your pow - er so great;
as we turn to your Word, we can see
at - tri - butes and your glo - ri - ous name,

More your great day will still re - late.
Your wis - dom shine so bril - liant - ly.
Ex - ult - ing - ly we will pro - claim.

(See also Ps. 36:9; 145:6-13; Jas. 1:17.)

2

We Thank You, Jehovah

(1 Thessalonians 5:18)

We thank you, Je - ho - vah, each day and each night,
We thank you, Je - ho - vah, for your lov - ing Son,
We thank you, our God, for the hon - or to preach

That you shed up - on us your pre - cious light.
Who con - quered the world; By his faith he won.
A - bout your great name and the truth to teach.

We thank you that we have the priv - 'lege of prayer,
We thank you for guid - ance in do - ing your will,
We thank you that soon all earth's woes will be past,

That we can ap - proach you with ev - 'ry care.
For thus you do help us our vows ful - fill.
While your King - dom bless - ings for - ev - er last.

(See also Ps. 50:14; 95:2; 147:7; Col. 3:15.)

3

"God Is Love"

(1 John 4:7, 8)

God is love, and he in-vites us, 'Walk with me and love my way.'
Love of truth moves us to ac-tion; Love of God moves us to love.
Nev-er let re-sent-ment lead you; May it nev-er take your hand.

When we love both God and neigh-bor, Gra-cious deeds will fill each day.
When we fail he seeks to help us; By his strength we rise a-bove.
Look to God, and he will guide you; He will teach you these com-mands:

There-in lies the key to liv-ing; There-in lies the life we seek.
Love is pure and nev-er jeal-ous; Love is kind and bears all things.
Love of God and love of neigh-bor, Ev-'ry-thing that love should be.

Christ-like love will nev-er fail us. Christ-like love through us will speak.
May we grow to love our broth-er. May we taste what true love brings.
May we al-ways show to oth-ers God-like love, yes, ten-der-ly.

(See also Mark 12:30, 31; 1 Cor. 12:31–13:8; 1 John 3:23.)

4 *Making a Good Name With God*

(Ecclesiastes 7:1)

Throughout our life-time,
We want to use each day
To make a good name
And all God's laws o-bey.
If in Je-ho-vah's sight
We strive to do what's right,
Then to his own heart
We'll bring de-light.

To seek in this world
A cel-e-brat-ed name,
To want its fa-vor,
To bask in its ac-claim
Is sim-ply van-i-ty.
For if its friend we'd be,
Je-ho-vah's fa-vor
We would not see.

In God's re-mem-brance
We want our name to be
In-scribed in his book
For all e-ter-ni-ty.
On him we can de-pend,
So we his truth de-fend
And keep our good name
Down to the end.

(See also Gen. 11:4; Prov. 22:1; Mal. 3:16; Rev. 20:15.)

5
Christ, Our Exemplar
(Romans 5:8)

What love Je-ho-vah showed, What bless-ings from him flowed,
Christ taught us ev-'ry day For God's great name to pray,
God's truth Christ Je-sus taught And ten-der com-fort brought

When for all man-kind he gave his dear Son.
The name Je-ho-vah to be sanc-ti-fied.
To those who fol-lowed as his faith-ful sheep.

Christ then be-came our bread, That we might all be fed,
Pray that his King-dom come And that his will be done.
May seeds of King-dom praise Be sown through all our days.

And life e-ter-nal in peace might be won.
Pray that he dai-ly our bread will pro-vide.
Then sat-is-fac-tion and joy we will reap.

(See also Matt. 6:9-11; John 3:16; 6:31-51; Eph. 5:2.)

6 *The Prayer of God's Servant*

(Ephesians 6:18)

Heav - en - ly Fa - ther, Sov - er - eign Lord, May your great name for-
Love for the truth with - in us in - still. Help us, O God, to
Wis - dom we seek from heav - en a - bove. Please grant this gift, and

ev - er be a - dored. Your ten - der mer - cies long will en - dure,
car - ry out your will. All your com - mand - ments we want to keep.
fill our hearts with love. Help us our love and mer - cy to show,

Ev - er so faith - ful, ev - er so sure. Ev - er faith - ful,
Find - ing and feed - ing your pre - cious sheep. Find - ing, feed - ing
Help - ing all men our great God to know. Help - ing all our

ev - er sure, All your mer - cies will en - dure.
your dear sheep, Your com - mands we want to keep.
God to know, May our love and mer - cy show.

(See also Ps. 143:10; John 21:15-17; Jas. 1:5.)

7 *Christian Dedication*

(Hebrews 10:7, 9)

Be-cause Je-ho-vah cre-at-ed The u-ni-verse so grand, To
In wa-ter Je-sus was bap-tized To righ-teous-ness ful-fill. In
We come be-fore you, Je-ho-vah, To praise your name so great. Dis-

him be-long the earth and sky, The works of his own hand. The
sol-emn prayer he said to God: 'I've come to do your will.' When
own-ing self, with hum-ble hearts Our lives we ded-i-cate. You

breath of life he has giv-en And to his crea-tures shown That
he came up from the Jor-dan As God's a-noint-ed Son, O-
gave your on-ly-be-got-ten, Who paid the price so high. No

wor-thy is he to have the praise, The wor-ship of all his own.
be-dient and loy-al he would serve As God's ded-i-cat-ed One.
lon-ger as liv-ing for our-selves, For you we shall live or die.

(See also Matt. 16:24; Mark 8:34; Luke 9:23.)

The Lord's Evening Meal

(Matthew 26:26-30)

Je - ho - vah, our Fa - ther in heav - en, Oh,
We're gath - ered to - geth - er be - fore you. As

this is a most sa - cred night! It was
sheep of your pas - ture, we came To give

Ni - san four - teen when your glo - ry was seen, Your
praise for your love that brought Christ from a - bove, To

love, jus - tice, wis - dom, and might. The
hon - or your most ho - ly name. We

The Lord's Evening Meal

Pass — o — ver lamb was then eat — en, And
keep this Me — mo — rial oc — ca — sion Fixed

Is — ra — el's tribes went forth free. Cen — t'ries
firm — ly in heart and in mind. Thus we'll

lat — er our Lord his own life — blood out — poured To ful —
walk ev — 'ry day as Christ showed us the way, And then

fill this di — vine proph — e — cy.
life ev — er — last — ing we'll find.

(See also Luke 22:14-20; 1 Cor. 11:23-26.)

Praise Jehovah, Our God!

(Psalm 145:12)

Praise our God! Praise Je-ho-vah God! Make his glo-rious name known to all! Sound a-larm! For his day is near, And all men must heed his warn-ing call. Our God has de-creed that now is the time For his

Praise our God! Sing it loud and clear! With a joy-ful song, laud his name! From the heart, From a grate-ful heart, All his glo-ry bold-ly we pro-claim. Though grand is our God and great are his works, He is

Praise Jehovah, Our God!

First-born to rule as King. Reach out to all men, and
humble and good to all. He shows loving-kindness,

tell them the news, Tell what blessings our God will bring! Praise our
mercy, and love And will hear when to him we call. Praise our

Chorus

God! Praise Jehovah God! Make his greatness known in all the earth!

(See also Ps. 89:27; 105:1; Jer. 33:11.)

"Here I Am! Send Me"

(Isaiah 6:8)

Today men heap re-proach and shame, In many ways on
Men make the taunt that God is slow; The fear of God they
Today the meek ones mourn and sigh Be-cause the e-vils

God's fair name. Some show God weak; some paint him cruel. "There
do not know. Some wor-ship i-dols made of stone; Some
mul-ti-ply. With hon-est hearts they seek to find The

is no God!" so shouts the fool. Who'll go the name of God to
would put Cae-sar on God's throne. Who'll tell the wick-ed what's in
truth that gives real peace of mind. Who'll go with com-fort to the

clear? Who'll sing his praise for all to hear? "Lord,
store? Who'll warn of God's great fi-nal war? "Lord,
meek? Who'll help them righ-teous-ness to seek? "Lord,

"Here I Am! Send Me"

here I am! Send me, send me. I'll sing your prais - es faith - ful - ly.
here I am! Send me, send me. I'll sound the warn - ing fear - less - ly.
here I am! Send me, send me. I'll teach such meek ones pa - tient - ly.

Chorus

No great - er hon - or could there be, Lord. Here I am! Send me, send me."

(See also Ps. 10:4; Ezek. 9:4.)

11 *Making Jehovah's Heart Glad*

(Proverbs 27:11)

Great God, we've vowed to do your will;
Your slave, your stew - ard here on earth,
Im - part to us your ac - tive force,

In wis - dom your work we'll ful - fill.
Pro - claims your great - ness and your worth,
That we may keep a faith - ful course

For then we know we'll have a part
Feeds us with nour - ish - ment when due,
And bring forth fruit - age to your praise

In mak - ing glad your lov - ing heart.
Thus strength - ens us your will to do.
And thus make glad your heart al - ways.

(See also Matt. 24:45-47; Luke 11:13; 22:42.)

12 *Life Everlasting Is Promised*

(Psalm 37:29)

Life ev - er - last - ing is prom - ised. Man's earth - ly home will en - dure.
Par - a - dise brought to per - fec - tion; All of God's chil - dren set free.
Soon in the grand res - ur - rec - tion, Sor - row will all dis - ap - pear.

'Meek ones will thrive,' said the psalm - ist. This grand fu - ture is sure.
Un - der Je - ho - vah's di - rec - tion, Peace on earth we will see.
Show - er - ing ten - der af - fec - tion, God will dry ev - 'ry tear.

Chorus

We can live for - ev - er. It's worth all en - deav - or.

God's prom - ise is faith - ful. His Word will come true.

(See also Isa. 25:8; Luke 23:43; John 11:25; Rev. 21:4.)

13

A Prayer of Thanksgiving

(Psalm 95:2)

Gra - cious Je - ho - vah, de - serv - ing of praise,
Hap - py are those whom you choose to in - vite
May your at - ten - tion cause joy to a - bound;

To you, O Sov - 'reign, our voic - es we raise.
In - to your courts of in - struc - tion and light.
In all the earth let your wor - ship be found.

We bow to you, O Great Hear - er of prayer,
Teach us to know you; your Word is our guide.
Crowned with your good - ness, your King - dom ap - pears,

Plac - ing our - selves un - der your ten - der care.
Here in your tem - ple, we wish to re - side.
Wip - ing out sick - ness, death, sor - row, and tears.

A Prayer of Thanksgiving

Dai - ly our er - rors re - veal we are weak;
Awe - some in - deed is your pow - er - ful hand,
All that is wick - ed, your Son will de - stroy;

For our trans - gres - sions for - give - ness we seek.
Giv - ing your ser - vants the cour - age to stand.
Bless - ed cre - a - tion will cry out for joy;

Look! with the blood of your Son we were bought.
God of sal - va - tion, your King - dom we hail.
Shout - ing in tri - umph, oh, thanks let us sing:

Now our de - sire is by you to be taught.
Preach it we must, for it nev - er will fail.
"Praise to Je - ho - vah, our glo - ri - ous King!"

(See also Ps. 65:2, 4, 11; Phil. 4:6.)

14

All Things Made New

(Revelation 21:1-5)

Chords (line 1): F7 Bb F/A Bb F7/C Bb/D Eb Cm7 F7

"The signs of the times" prove God's rule has be - gun. In
Let all men the chaste New Je - ru - sa - lem see, The
This cit - y so fair will be all men's de - light. Its

Chords (line 2): Bb F Bb F/A F2/C F Gm C13 F F/Eb

glo - ry en - throned sits Je - ho - vah's Son. The
bride of the Lamb shin - ing ra - diant - ly. A -
gates will be o - pen both day and night. All

Chords (line 3): Bb/D F F#° Gm D+5 D7 Gm C#°

bat - tle in heav - en he's fought and won, And
dorned now with most pre - cious gems is she, And
na - tions will walk in her glo - ry bright; O

Chords (line 4): Dm Dm/F Bb7 A7sus4 A7 Dm

soon on the earth shall God's will be done.
on - ly Je - ho - vah her light will be.
ser - vants of God, now re - flect that light.

All Things Made New

(See also Matt. 16:3; Rev. 12:7-9; 21:23-25.)

15 *Creation Reveals Jehovah's Glory*

(Psalm 19)

Je - ho - vah God, my soul is well a-
For you have made the sun and moon and
Your laws are pure, and your com - mands are

ware. A host of stars, your
stars. Great o - ceans stop where
true. Day af - ter day, re -

glo - ry does de - clare. From day to
you have set their bars. We lift our
mind - ers come from you. They make us

day and night to night they speak
eyes and see your heav - ens grand.
wise, are bet - ter than fine gold.

Creation Reveals Jehovah's Glory

(See also Ps. 12:6; 89:7; 144:3; Rom. 1:20.)

16

Flee to God's Kingdom!

(Zephaniah 2:3)

Oh, seek Jehovah, you meek ones and lowly;
Come, you who hunger for truth and for justice;
Look up, yes, lift up your heads with rejoicing;

Seek what is right, and seek meekness today.
Why longer sorrow and cry out in pain?
See all the proof that the Kingdom is here!

Thus it may be in the day of his anger That
Seek now God's way to escape the oppressor, Sub-
Welcome the light that Jehovah is sending, And

you may be hidden away.
mitting yourself to Christ's reign.
let him alone be your fear!

Flee to God's Kingdom!

(See also Ps. 59:16; Prov. 18:10; 1 Cor. 16:13.)

17

Forward, You Witnesses!

(Luke 16:16)

1. Firm and de-ter-mined in this time of the end, Pre-
pared are God's ser-vants the good news to de-fend. Though
Sa-tan a-gainst us has vaunt-ed, In our
God's strength we move a-head un-daunt-ed.

2. Sol-diers of Jah do not seek a life of ease; The
world and its rul-ers we do not try to please. Un-
spot-ted at all times re-main-ing, Our in-
teg-ri-ty we shall keep main-tain-ing.

3. God's King-dom hope has been mocked and pushed a-side; His
great name is slan-dered, its ho-li-ness de-nied. Let's
share in its sanc-ti-fi-ca-tion, And pro-
claim it to ev-'ry tribe and na-tion.

Chorus

Then

Forward, You Witnesses!

for - ward, you Wit - ness - es, ev - er strong of heart! Re -
joice that in God's work, you too may have a part! Go
tell far and wide that the par - a - dise is near And that
soon all its bless - ings will be here.

(See also Phil. 1:7; 2 Tim. 2:3, 4; Jas. 1:27.)

God's Loyal Love

(Isaiah 55:1-3)

Loy - al love! God is love. This truth cheers us
Loy - al love! God is love. All his works give
Loy - al love! God is love. May his love move

from a - bove. Love caused God to send his Son,
proof there - of. Love for us he's fur - ther shown,
us to love. Loy - al - ly we'll help the meek,

Who for us the ran - som won, That we might gain
Giv - ing Christ the king - ly throne To ful - fill his
As God's right - teous way they seek. May we preach with

righ - teous - ness, Life e - ter - nal,
cov - 'nant sworn. See! His King - dom
god - ly fear, Com - fort spread for

God's Loyal Love

(See also Ps. 33:5; 57:10; Eph. 1:7.)

19 *God's Promise of Paradise*

(Luke 23:43)

A par - a - dise our God has prom - ised, By means of
Soon here on earth, as God has pur - posed, His Son will
Yes, Par - a - dise, our Lord did prom - ise. And he is

Christ's Mil - len - nial Reign, When he'll blot out all sin and
cause the dead to rise. Thus it will be as Je - sus
now earth's right - ful King. We dai - ly thank our lov - ing

er - ror, Re - mov - ing death and tears and
prom - ised: 'You'll be with me in Par - a -
Fa - ther, And from our hearts, his prais - es

Chorus

pain. A par - a - dise, the earth will be. With eyes of
dise.'
sing.

faith, this we can see. This prom - ise Christ shall soon ful-

fill, For he de - lights to do God's will.

(See also Matt. 5:5; 6:10; John 5:28, 29.)

20 *Bless Our Meeting Together*
(Hebrews 10:24, 25)

Bless us as we meet to - geth - er, Great Je - ho - vah, we now pray.
Help us, Lord, re - fine our wor - ship; With your Word, oh, do us fill.
So, dear Fa - ther, bless our meet - ings; Grant us peace and u - ni - ty.

For our meet - ings we do thank you; May your spir - it with us stay.
Train our minds and tongues to wit - ness; Love with - in our hearts in - still.
May our words and may our ac - tions Mag - ni - fy your Sov - 'reign - ty.

(See also Ps. 22:22; 34:3; Isa. 50:4.)

21

Happy, the Merciful!

(Matthew 5:7)

How hap - py are the mer - ci - ful! In
Those mer - ci - ful like God are blessed; Through
The meek will see Je - ho - vah's love When

God's eyes they are beau - ti - ful. They
sins for - giv - en they have rest. They
they are judged by him a - bove. His

tell to all who love the right That
ben - e - fit by mer - cy shown, Since
mer - cy they will real - ly know, Since

God in mer - cy takes de - light. Through
Christ ap - peared be - fore God's throne. This
they, like him, true mer - cy show. So

Happy, the Merciful!

Je - sus, mer - cy God dis - played, Pro-
mer - cy they would glad - ly share By
mer - ci - ful let's strive to be And

vi - sion for our ran - som made. He
preach - ing God's Word ev - 'ry - where, By
cul - ti - vate that qual - i - ty. Our

of - fers mer - cy to the meek Be -
tell - ing men, "Be of good cheer Be -
God and Christ have shown the way; May

cause he knows our frame is weak.
cause the King - dom now is here."
we show mer - cy ev - 'ry day.

(See also Luke 6:36; Rom. 12:8; Jas. 2:13.)

22

"Jehovah Is My Shepherd"

(Psalm 23)

Je- ho- vah God is my Shep- herd; So why should I fear or
A- lone in depths of deep shad- ow, I walk, yet I fear no
How wise and lov- ing my Shep- herd! His prais- es with joy I

fret? For he who cares for his sheep so much Will
harm. For my Great Shep- herd is al - ways near; His
sing. The cheer- ing news of his ten - der care To

none of his own for - get. By qui - et wa - ters he
staff keeps me from a - larm. My head with oil he re -
sheep- like ones I will bring. His Word I'll faith- ful- ly

leads me, My soul does re - store and bless. He
fresh - es; My cup he has filled up well. His
fol - low, Walk care- ful- ly in his way. My

"Jehovah Is My Shepherd"

guides my steps for his own name's sake In
lov - ing - kind - ness will fol - low me, And
glo - rious trea - sure of serv - ing him, I'll

path - ways of righ - teous - ness. He
there in his house I'll dwell. His
grate - ful - ly use each day. My

guides my steps for his own name's sake In
lov - ing - kind - ness will fol - low me, And
glo - rious trea - sure of serv - ing him, I'll

path - ways of righ - teous - ness.
there in his house I'll dwell.
grate - ful - ly use each day.

(See also Ps. 28:9; 80:1.)

23 *Jehovah, Our Strength*

(Isaiah 12:2)

Gra- cious Je - ho - vah, our strength and our might,
We who now serve you re - joice in your light;
Glad - ly, O God, we keep do - ing your will.

You are our Sav - ior, in you we de - light.
With o - pened eyes, we now see truth and right.
Though Sa - tan mocks us, we're trust - ing you still.

We are your Wit - ness - es bear - ing your news,
Search - ing the Scrip - tures, we hear your com - mand;
Though he may slay us, oh, help us to be

Wheth - er men hear or they proud - ly re - fuse.
Mak - ing our choice, for your King - dom we stand. Je -
Firm to the end for your grand Sov - 'reign - ty.

Chorus

Jehovah, Our Strength

ho - vah, our Rock, our strength and our might,

Your name we make known both day and night.

Glo - rious Je - ho - vah, Al - migh - ty in pow'r,

You are our hid - ing place; You are our Tow'r.

(See also 2 Sam. 22:3; Ps. 18:2; Isa. 43:12.)

Keep Your Eyes on the Prize!

(2 Corinthians 4:18)

When eyes of blind ones see a — gain And
When tongues of mute ones speak a — gain, When
When wolves and lambs will feed as one, When

ears of deaf ones hear a — gain, When
old ones will be young a — gain, When
bears and calves bask in the sun, A

des — erts blos — som as the rose And
earth will yield her rich in — crease And
mere young boy will lead them all, And

from parched ground fresh wa — ter flows, When
all good things will nev — er cease, When
they will heed his child — ish call. When

Keep Your Eyes on the Prize!

F	F+5	Dm/F	C/Bb	Bb	D7/A

lame ones leap just like the hart, When
songs of chil - dren fill the air, When
tears be - long to yes - ter - day, When

Gm		Eb/G	Gm6(ma7)	C7sus4		C7

loved ones nev - er have to part, Such
joy and peace are ev - 'ry - where, Then,
fears and pain have passed a - way, You'll

F		Cm7	A+5	Bb	F/A	Bbm/G

bless - ed times you'll re - al - ize, If
too, you'll see the dead a - rise, If
see how God these things sup - plies, If

F/C	F/A	Db7/Ab	Gm7	Bb/C	C7	F

you keep your eyes on the prize.
you keep your eyes on the prize.
you keep your eyes on the prize.

(See also Isa. 11:6-9; 35:5-7; John 11:24.)

25 *Proof of Discipleship*

(John 13:34, 35)

There is a law we must all o - bey
Gen - u - ine love that will nev - er fail

If we would live the Chris - tian way.
Ten - der - ly aids the weak or frail.

This is the king - ly law from a - bove;
Love is a debt that we must re - pay,

This is how we show Christ - like love.
Serv - ing will - ing - ly day by day.

Proof of Discipleship

Such was the love of our Lord, the Christ;
No oth-er place could we ev-er find

His per-fect life he sac-ri-ficed.
Friends show-ing love of this rare kind.

He left a mod-el we fol-low close-ly;
These are the bonds that we can be sure of;

His dis-ci-ples, we prove to be.
May we fol-low the way of love.

(See also Rom. 13:8; 1 Cor. 13:8; Jas. 2:8; 1 John 4:10, 11.)

26

Oh, Walk With God!

(Micah 6:8)

Oh, walk with God in mod - es - ty;
Oh, walk with God in pu - ri - ty;
Oh, walk with God in faith - ful - ness,

Love kind - ness, and be true.
Re - lapse not in - to sin.
For then you will at - tain

With God keep your in - teg - ri - ty;
Ad - vance to full ma - tu - ri - ty;
Con - tent - ment true and god - li - ness,

Let him your strength re - new.
And his ap - prov - al win.
Which are the great - est gain.

Oh, Walk With God!

If you would keep his truth so grand,
And on what- ev - er things are pure
Oh, walk with God; be ev - er glad

By men be not be - guiled;
And love - ly, true, and just,
His glo - rious praise to sing.

But let God lead you by the hand,
On these things think; and to en - dure,
The great - est joy that can be had,

Just as a lit - tle child.
In God put all your trust.
His King - dom work will bring.

(See also Gen. 5:24; 6:9; Phil. 4:8; 1 Tim. 6:6-8.)

27 *Take Sides With Jehovah!*

(Exodus 32:26)

Once with con - fu - sion our sad hearts were filled,
Now we're re - joic - ing in serv - ing our God,
We will not fear what the Dev - il can do.

Drink - ing the cup false re - li - gion dis - tilled;
Spread - ing the seeds of his truth all a - broad,
Trust - ing Je - ho - vah will car - ry us through.

But with what hap - pi - ness our hearts were thrilled
Help - ing our broth - ers God's vir - tues to laud,
Though they are man - y and though we are few,

When of God's King - dom we heard.
Prais - ing his great wor - thy name.
God is our strength and our might.

Take Sides With Jehovah!

Take sides with Jehovah; Make him your delight. He'll never forsake you; Walk on in his light. Tell, tell the glad tidings Of freedom and peace. His rule by Christ Jesus Will ever increase.

(See also Ps. 94:14; Prov. 3:5, 6; Heb. 13:5.)

28
The New Song
(Psalm 98)

The New Song

In the cause of jus - tice, He judg - es righ - teous - ly.
Harp and horn and trum - pet Sound praise in full ac - cord.
Moun - tains, hills, and val - leys Sing praise in all the lands.

Chorus

Sing, sing, sing! The new song, let it ring! Sing, sing, sing! Je - ho - vah is our King.

(See also Ps. 96:1; 149:1; Isa. 42:10.)

Walking in Integrity
(Psalm 26)

Please, judge me, Lord, / observe my loy-al-ty;
I / do not sit / with wick-ed men of lies.
For / I have loved / the dwell-ing of your house.

Ob-serve my trust in you / and my in-
I hate the com-pa-ny / of those who
Your wor-ship, oh, so pure, / I dai-ly

teg-ri-ty. / Ex-am-ine me, and
truth de-spise. / With e-vil men, take
will es-pouse. / And I will march a-

put me to the test; / My mind and heart re-
not a-way my life; / My soul, with those whose
round your al-tar grand, / To make thanks-giv-ing

Walking in Integrity

fine,   that   my   soul   might   be   blessed.
hands   are   full   of   bribes   and   strife.
heard   a - loud   through - out   the   land.   But

as   for   me,   De - ter - mined   I   shall   be   to   walk   e -

ter - nal - ly   In   my   in - teg - ri - ty.

(See also Ps. 25:2.)

30

Jehovah Begins His Rule

(Revelation 11:15)

This is a glo-ri-ous day. God's rule is now un-der way.
Christ now in pow-er is here, And Ar-ma-ged-don is near.
God's reign-ing Rul-er we prize. Won-drous he is in our eyes.

He's laid in Zi-on his Chief Cor-ner-stone.
Sa-tan's old sys-tem will soon pass a-way.
He comes in God's name; we bow to our King.

Let all now lift up the voice. Sing to our God, and re-joice.
Now is the sea-son to preach. Man-y there are yet to reach;
En-ter the grand tem-ple gate; God's fa-vor now sup-pli-cate.

Christ, Lord and Sav-ior, has been placed up-on His throne.
Time for the meek to take their stand for Him to-day.
Soon dawns that day when he rules o-ver ev-'ry-thing.

Jehovah Begins His Rule

Chorus

What will you bring, Je - ho - vah's King - dom? Tri - umph of truth and righ - teous - ness. And bring what else, Je - ho - vah's King - dom? E - ter - nal life and hap - pi - ness. Praise the U - ni - ver - sal Sov - 'reign For his love and faith - ful - ness.

(See also 2 Sam. 7:22; Dan. 2:44; Rev. 7:15.)

31
We Are Jehovah's Witnesses!
(Isaiah 43:10-12)

Men make gods of wood and stone, But the true God
Proud-ly we de-clare God's name, Bear-ing wit-ness
Wit-ness-ing ex-alts God's name, Lifts there-from re-

they've not known. He is God Al-might-y,
to his fame. News a-bout his King-dom,
proach and shame. And it warns the wick-ed,

As he's of-ten shown. Oth-er gods just can-not see
Bold-ly we pro-claim. Oth-ers thus may come to see
Who God's name de-fame. Par-don it holds out to men,

What in fu-ture days will be. For wit-ness-es they
Truth from God that sets them free. As they grow strong, their
If they turn to God a-gain. Thus bear-ing wit-ness

We Are Jehovah's Witnesses!

look all in vain, Since none their god - ship
voic - es they'll raise, Join - ing with us to
brings joy and peace And hope of life that

can main - tain.
sing his praise.   We're Je - ho - vah's Wit - ness - es.
will not cease.

We speak out in fear - less - ness. Ours is the God of

true proph - e - cy; What he fore - tells comes to be.

(See also Isa. 37:19; 55:11; Ezek. 3:19.)

Be Steadfast, Unmovable!

(1 Corinthians 15:58)

Na - tions are trou - bled as nev - er be - fore.
Snares of this world and temp - ta - tions a - bound.
Give to God wor - ship that comes from the heart.

Peo - ple are fear - ful of what lies in store.
We can re - sist if our think - ing is sound.
In the Lord's ser - vice may we have a part.

Firm and un - mov - a - ble we need to be,
If we hold fast to what God says is true,
Preach the good news, al - ways hold - ing it fast.

Serv - ing our God faith - ful - ly.
Safe - ly he'll car - ry us through.
Soon the last days will have passed.

Be Steadfast, Unmovable!

Stead - fast we all need to be;
Far from this world we keep free,
As we feed on God's truth and keep in -
teg - ri - ty.

(See also Luke 21:9; 1 Pet. 4:7.)

33

Fear Them Not!

(Matthew 10:28)

Ev - er on - ward, O my peo - ple, Let the King - dom tid - ings go.
E - ven though your foes are man - y, Though they threat - en and re - vile,
Nev - er fear you are for - got - ten; I am still your strength and shield.

Trem - ble not be - fore our foe. Let all lov - ers of truth know
Though they flat - ter and they smile, To mis - lead and to be - guile,
Though you die up - on the field, E - ven death to me will yield.

That my reign - ing Son, Christ Je - sus, To the earth has cast the foe,
Fear them not, my faith - ful war - riors, Nor their per - se - cu - tion's heat,
Fear them not who kill the bod - y But can - not de - stroy the soul.

Soon to bind the Dev - il, Sa - tan, Let - ting all his vic - tims go.
For I will pre - serve the faith - ful Till the vic - t'ry is com - plete.
To the end may you be faith - ful; I will bring you to your goal!

Fear Them Not!

Chorus

Fear them not, O my be - lov - ed,
Though their boast - ing threats may fly.
I will keep my faith - ful ser - vant
As the ap - ple of my eye.

(See also Deut. 32:10; Neh. 4:14; Ps. 59:1; 83:2, 3.)

34 *Living Up to Our Name*

(Isaiah 43:10-12)

Glo - rious Je - ho - vah, al - might - y, e - ter - nal,
Work - ing to - geth - er in your sa - cred ser - vice

Per - fect in jus - tice, in pow - er, in love.
Binds us as broth - ers in love and in peace.

Source of all truth and of in - fi - nite wis - dom,
Teach - ing the truth and re - flect - ing your glo - ry

You rule as Sov - 'reign in heav - en a - bove.
Fill us with joy as your prais - es in - crease.

Living Up to Our Name

We as your people delight in your service;
Known by your name, O Jehovah, our Father,

Your Kingdom truth we delight to proclaim.
We have the honor to add to your fame.

Chorus

Being your Witnesses, great is our priv'lege.

Oh, may we ever live up to our name!

(See also Deut. 32:4; Ps. 43:3; Dan. 2:20, 21.)

35 *Gratitude for Divine Patience*

(2 Peter 3:15)

Great God, Je - ho - vah, bound - less in might,
One thou - sand years, from your point of view,

You have made known your love of right.
Are like a day when they are through.

Wick - ed - ness rules on earth be - low,
Time now pro - ceeds to your great day;

Caus - ing you pain, as we well know.
It will ar - rive with - out de - lay.

Gratitude for Divine Patience

You are not slow, as men may contend;
Though all trans-gres-sion you do re-sent,
Your time is near for bad-ness to end.
Your heart is glad when sin-ners re-pent.
We look to you in hope and trust,
We look a-head with hope re-newed,
Grate-ful that you are pa-tient and just.
Prais-ing your name in deep grat-i-tude.

(See also Luke 15:7; 2 Pet. 3:8, 9.)

36 *"What God Has Yoked Together"*

(Matthew 19:5, 6)

With dig-ni-ty and joy, A three-fold cord is bound.
They both have searched God's Word To learn to do his will,

With God and men to wit-ness, These sa-cred vows re-sound.
And now they seek his bless-ing, Their prom-ise to ful-fill.

He vowed be-fore Je-ho-vah To love her from the heart.
She vowed be-fore Je-ho-vah To love him from the heart.

Chorus

"What God has yoked to-geth-er Let no man put a-part."

(See also Gen. 2:24; Eccl. 4:12; Eph. 5:22-33.)

37 *The Scriptures—Inspired of God*

(2 Timothy 3:16, 17)

God's Word is a shin- ing light,
That di - vine Word is in - spired,
By these Scrip- tures from a - bove,

Guides our feet through earth's dark night.
Teach - es us what is re - quired.
We have come to know God's love.

If we fol - low it faith - ful - ly,
Help it gives, set- ting all things straight,
Read - ing dai - ly will make us wise,

Sure - ly its truth will set us free.
And for God's dis - ci - pline to wait.
Show- ing us how to gain life's prize.

(See also Ps. 119:105; Prov. 4:13.)

38 *Throw Your Burden on Jehovah*

(Psalm 55)

Please give ear, O Lord, Je - ho - vah,
Had I wings just as a dove has,
I will call up - on Je - ho - vah,

Let your - self be found by me.
Far from dan - ger I would fly,
His pro - tec - tion I will seek.

Hear my prayer, and may you an - swer,
Safe from those who seek to hurt me,
He gives peace midst op - po - si - tion;

Help me un - a - fraid to be.
Shel - tered from their hate - ful cry.
Strength he gives to all the meek.

Throw Your Burden on Jehovah

(See also Ps. 22:5; 31:1-24.)

39 *Our Possession of Peace*

(John 14:27)

Praise Je-ho-vah, God of peace, God of u-ni-ty.
We have left off an-gry words, Mak-ing quar-rels cease.
As a fruit of righ-teous-ness, Peace we all must bear,

He will make all wars to cease, Bring in har-mo-ny.
We have made from spears and swords, Im-ple-ments of peace.
Proof of wis-dom from a-bove, Gained through heart-felt prayer.

Prince of Peace is Christ his Son, Ten-der, calm, and kind.
If this peace we want to keep, Then we must for-give.
We would rec-om-mend our way, Show our peace-ful care

When the fight for right he's won, Per-fect peace we'll find.
Peace-ful-ly as Je-sus' sheep, May we learn and live.
Till the King-dom's per-fect day Brings peace ev-'ry-where.

(See also Ps. 46:9; Isa. 2:4; Jas. 3:17, 18.)

40 *Keep On Seeking First the Kingdom*

(Matthew 6:33)

Some-thing pre - cious to Je - ho - vah, Bring-ing him such keen de -
Why be anx - ious for to - mor - row Lest we hun - ger, lest we
So pro - claim the King - dom good news; Help de - serv - ing ones to

light, Is his King-dom by Christ Je - sus, Which will set all mat - ters
thirst? For our God will make pro - vi - sion If we seek his King-dom
see That their hope is in Je - ho - vah And in his The - oc - ra -

Chorus

right.
first. Keep on seek - ing first the King-dom And Je - ho - vah's right-teous-
cy.

ness. Sing his praise a-mong the na - tions, Serv-ing him in faith-ful - ness.

(See also Ps. 27:14; Matt. 6:34; 10:11, 13; 1 Pet. 1:21.)

41 *Worship Jehovah During Youth*

(Ecclesiastes 12:1)

Pre - cious to God are you daugh - ters and sons;
Great his af - fec - tion for you, our dear ones.

Hon - or your par - ents who care for your life,
Giv - ing no cause for con - ten - tion or strife.

Al - ways re - mem - ber your God in your youth;
Grow ev - er stron - ger in love of the truth.

Lov - ing at - ten - tion to you he ex - tends
If you gain fa - vor with God and with men,
By your de - vo - tion to God you will bring

Through us, your par - ents, your fam - 'ly, and friends.
Days of your youth will be hap - pi - est then.
Joy to the heart of Je - ho - vah, our King.

(See also Ps. 71:17; Lam. 3:27; Eph. 6:1-3.)

42   "Assist Those Who Are Weak"

(Acts 20:35)

Man-y are the weak-ness-es That we all pos-sess.
'Who is weak, and I'm not weak?' Paul did em-pa-thize.
Rath-er than con-demn the weak, We should bear in mind

Still Je-ho-vah cares for us, Loves us none-the-less.
With Christ's blood we all were bought, Life to re-al-ize.
How much we can strength-en them By our be-ing kind.

He is so mer-ci-ful; His love, so pow-er-ful.
Weak ones to God be-long, Hence he can make them strong.
May we be dil-i-gent, Give them en-cour-age-ment;

May we too dis-play such love, Help those in dis-tress.
May we feel their pain and cares, Help them dry their eyes.
As we lend our kind sup-port, Com-fort they will find.

(See also 2 Cor. 11:29; Isa. 35:3, 4; Gal. 6:2.)

43 *Stay Awake, Stand Firm, Grow Mighty*

(1 Corinthians 16:13)

Verse 1:
Stay a-wake, stand firm, grow might-y, Be de-ter-mined to en-dure. Car-ry on as men of cour-age, For the vic-to-ry is sure. We o-

Verse 2:
Stay a-wake, and keep your sens-es, Al-ways read-y to o-bey. Stay a-lert to Christ's di-rec-tion Through his faith-ful slave to-day. Heed the

Verse 3:
Stay a-wake, re-main u-nit-ed As the good news we de-fend. Though our en-e-mies will fight it, We will preach un-til the end. Join the

Stay Awake, Stand Firm, Grow Mighty

bey Christ Je - sus' clear com - mand, Un - der
coun - sel of the old - er men, Who pro -
shout of praise through - out the land. Look! Je -

him we firm - ly take our stand.
tect his sheep and truth de - fend. Stay a -
ho - vah's day is soon at hand!

wake, stand firm, and grow might - y! Car - ry

on right to the end!

(See also Matt. 24:13; Heb. 13:7, 17; 1 Pet. 5:8.)

Sharing Joyfully in the Harvest

(Matthew 13:1-23)

We live in the time of the har - vest, A
True love for our God and our neigh - bor Now

priv - 'lege be - yond all com - pare. God's
moves us to speed up our pace. Both

glo - ri - ous an - gels are reap - ers; In
har - vest and preach - ing are ur - gent, For

this work we too have a share. Christ
short - ly the end we will face. The

Sharing Joyfully in the Harvest

Je - sus has set the ex - am - ple By
joy we re - ceive is sur - pass - ing; As

tak - ing the lead in the field. So
God's fel - low work - ers, we share. So

great is the hon - or be - stowed on us To
may we en - dure in his King - dom work And

joy - ful - ly share in his yield.
know that his bless - ing is there.

(See also Matt. 24:13; 1 Cor. 3:9; 2 Tim. 4:2.)

45

Move Ahead!

(Hebrews 6:1)

Move a - head, move a - head to ma - tu - ri - ty!
Move a - head, move a - head, bold - ly wit - ness - ing!
Move a - head, move a - head, al - ways fol - low through,

It's the will of our God that we gain a - bil - i - ty.
Ev - er - last - ing good news to all sorts of peo - ple bring.
And im - prove in your skills for there's so much work to do.

Try your best to im - prove in your min - is - try,
Join in praise to Je - ho - vah, our God and King,
Let God's spir - it keep on mo - ti - vat - ing you.

Then our God your work will bless.
As we preach from door to door.
Find the joy that is di - vine.

Move Ahead!

There's a place in the ser - vice for all.
Wick - ed foes try to cause us to fear.
Love the peo - ple you work hard to find.

It's the work Je - sus did, you'll re - call.
Don't shrink back, but let ev - 'ry - one hear
Keep re - turn - ing to reach heart and mind.

Look to God that you thus at no time may fall,
Joy - ful news that the King - dom of God is here.
And as - sist all good prog - ress each day to make,

Stand - ing firm for righ - teous - ness.
Teach the truth yet more and more.
So the light of truth will shine.

(See also Phil. 1:27; 3:16; Heb. 10:39.)

46

Jehovah Is Our King!

(Psalm 97:1)

Re- joice, give glo- ry to Je- ho- vah, For the
His glo- ry tell a- mong the na- tions; Of his
His righ- teous rule is now es- tab- lished. On his

heav- ens have told forth his righ- teous- ness. Let us
great sav- ing acts tell from day to day. For Je-
throne, he has placed his a- noint- ed Son. Let the

sing to our God joy- ful songs to his praise And con-
ho- vah is King; He de- serves all the praise. We bow
gods of this world suf- fer shame and bow down, For the

cern our- selves with his great acts.
down be- fore his might- y throne.
praise be- longs to God a- lone. Let the

Jehovah Is Our King!

heav- ens re-joice, Let the earth joy-ful be, For Je-

ho- vah has be-come our King! Let the

heav- ens re-joice, Let the earth joy-ful be, For Je-

ho- vah has be- come our King!

(See also 1 Chron. 16:9; Ps. 68:20; 97:6, 7.)

47 *Declare the Good News*

(Revelation 14:6, 7)

The full - ness of the King - dom truth was long con - cealed. The
The good news that we now de - clare was long fore - known. Je -

truth a - bout the prom - ised Seed is now re - vealed. Je -
ho - vah wills that in this time it shall be shown. A -

ho - vah in his mer - cy and his love of right, Con -
long with us, his an - gels take de - light to share, To

sid - ered man's con - di - tion in his sin - ful plight. He
aid us as the King - dom truth we now de - clare. We

Declare the Good News

formed his pur - pose that his Son should rule the earth; In
have the du - ty and the hon - or in these days To

God's due time the King - dom rule would be brought to birth. And
sanc - ti - fy his name and give him his right - ful praise. We're

that he might ar - range to bring his Son a bride, A
hon - ored as his Wit - ness - es that name to bear With

lit - tle flock of cho - sen ones is glo - ri - fied.
ev - er - last - ing good news that we now de - clare.

(See also Mark 4:11; Acts 5:31; 1 Cor. 2:1, 7.)

48 *Daily Walking With Jehovah*

(Micah 6:8)

Hand in hand with our dear Fa-ther, We would
In this day of man-kind's judg-ment, As the
Help for us God has pro-vid-ed Through his

hum-bly walk with him each day. Oh, how
sys-tem's end is draw-ing near, We are
spir-it and his writ-ten Word, Through the

un-de-served his kind-ness That he
faced with op-po-si-tion That could
Chris-tian con-gre-ga-tion, Through as-

grants to those who seek his way! God for
make us turn a-way in fear. But Je-
sur-ance that our prayer is heard. As we're

Daily Walking With Jehovah

(See also Gen. 5:24; 6:9; 1 Ki. 2:3, 4.)

49

Jehovah Is Our Refuge

(Psalm 91)

Je - ho - vah is our ref - uge, Our
Though thou - sands will be fall - ing A -
Pro - tec - tion God will give you From

God in whom we trust. His shad - ow is our
long your ver - y side, A - mong those who are
snares a - long your way, And nev - er will you

shel - ter; A - bide in it we must. For
loy - al, In safe - ty you'll re - side. You
fal - ter In fear or in dis - may. The

he him - self will us de - fend, Up -
will not need to quake with fear, As
maned young li - on, you'll not dread; Up -

Jehovah Is Our Refuge

on   his   might   we   can   de - pend.   Je -
though   great   harm   to   you   were   near.   Your
on   the   co - bra   you   will   tread.   Je -

ho - vah   is   a   strong - hold,   Giv - ing
eyes   will   mere - ly   see   it,   Un - der -
ho - vah   is   our   ref - uge,   Ev - er

shel - ter   to   all   the   just.
neath   God's   wings   you'll   a - bide.
guard - ing   us   on   our   way.

(See also Ps. 97:10; 121:3, 5; Isa. 52:12.)

50 *The Divine Pattern of Love*

(1 John 4:19)

Je-ho-vah our God has wise-ly pro-vid-ed For us
When we walk God's way, our love for our broth-er Will be
Our love for our God im-pels us to serve him All our

all, One and all, A pat-tern of
true, Warm and true; Will make us a-
days, All our days. We glad-ly o-

love, that we may be guid-ed, Lest we should
lert to help one an-oth-er In all we
bey with heart-felt de-vo-tion, Sing-ing his

fall, Lest we should fall. Come fol-low God's
do, In all we do; Will help us for-
praise, Sing-ing his praise. So may we pro-

The Divine Pattern of Love

way, so warm and in - vit - ing; The way that is
give each small im - per - fec - tion, Will help us to
claim his name to each hear - er; May they come to

right, to fine works in - cit - ing; The road - way to
have true ten - der af - fec - tion, Will help us to
see the truth ev - er clear - er. May his ser - vice

peace, God's peo - ple u - nit - ing. God's way is
be our Fa - ther's re - flec - tion, Show - ing our
grow still dear - er and dear - er, For that is

love. Yes, God's way is love.
love, Our broth - er - ly love.
love. Yes, that is true love.

(See also Rom. 12:10; Eph. 4:3; 2 Pet. 1:7.)

51 *We Cleave to Jehovah*

(Joshua 23:8)

Our Sov - 'reign, Je - ho - vah, has shown him - self de -
On truth and on jus - tice his throne is firm - ly
The heav - en of heav - ens it - self can - not con -

serv - ing. In all of his deal - ings, his
found - ed. The place of his dwell - ing with
tain him. No foe can re - sist him, no

jus - tice is un - swerv - ing. No word he has
glo - ry is sur - round - ed. At his in - vi -
en - e - my re - strain him. All things he has

spo - ken will prove to be in vain. We
ta - tion, to him the meek now stream. We
prom - ised, we trust him to ful - fill. We

We Cleave to Jehovah

cleave to Je - ho - vah and close to him re -
cleave to Je - ho - vah, the God who is su -
cleave to Je - ho - vah; We want to do his

main; Em - brac - ing his rule is the
preme; De - serv - ing is he of our
will, And may our de - vo - tion to

way of last - ing gain.
wor - ship - ful es - teem.
him grow deep - er still.

(See also Deut. 4:4; 30:20; 2 Ki. 18:6; Ps. 89:14.)

Guard Your Heart

(Proverbs 4:23)

Oh, guard your heart, it means your life;
Pre - pare your heart to search for God
Pro - tect your heart from harm - ful thoughts;

A - void the path of sin.
By means of ear - nest prayer.
Con - sid - er what is true.

God reads the heart, and there he finds
With con - stan - cy, give praise and thanks;
Al - low God's Word to reach your heart,

The per - son deep with - in.
Con - fide each need and care.
To strength - en and re - new.

Guard Your Heart

Sometimes the heart is des - per - ate
The things Je - ho - vah teach - es us
Je - ho - vah loves his loy - al ones;

And could be - gin to stray.
Are things we should o - bey.
On this we can de - pend.

So use your mind to guide your heart,
So cul - ti - vate a loy - al heart,
So wor - ship him whole - heart - ed - ly

And keep Je - ho - vah's way.
And please him ev - 'ry day.
For - ev - er as his friend.

(See also Ps. 34:1; Phil. 4:8; 1 Pet. 3:4.)

53 *Working Together in Unity*

(Ephesians 4:3)

Working Together in Unity

ny is sweet. In God's work there's
such de - light. As we show true

much to be done. He di - rects us now through his
broth - er - ly love, God will grant us peace from a -

Son. May we serve o - be - di - ent -
bove. With his help, u - nit - ed we'll

ly, Work - ing in har - mo - ny.
be, Serv - ing him end - less - ly.

(See also Mic. 2:12; Zeph. 3:9; 1 Cor. 1:10.)

54 *We Must Have the Faith*

(Hebrews 10:38, 39)

On	man - y oc - ca - sions	God spoke to men	By
We	glad - ly o - bey	Christ Je - sus' com - mand	To
Our	faith is an an - chor	firm and se - cure;	We

means of his proph - ets of old.	To -
share King - dom truth far and wide.	We
nev - er will shrink back in fear.	Though

day he has said, 'Let all men re - pent,'	By
care - ful - ly guard our free - ness of speech;	This
en - e - mies will a - gainst us a - rise,	We

God's own Son we are told.	Do we
truth we nev - er will hide.	
know sal - va - tion is near.	

Chorus

We Must Have the Faith

have the faith that is sure? We must build such faith to sur - vive. Is our faith proved true by our works? This kind of faith pre - serves our souls a - live.

(See also Rom. 10:10; Eph. 3:12; Heb. 11:6; 1 John 5:4.)

55 *Life Without End—At Last!*

(John 3:16)

Can you see with your mind's eye, Peo - ples dwell - ing to - geth - er?
In those days old will grow young, Flesh re - vived as in child - hood.
Par - a - dise all will en - joy As we sing of God's glo - ry.

Sor - row has passed. Peace at last! Life with - out tears or pain.
Trou - bles are gone, from now on, No need to weep or fear.
Long as we live, we will give To God, our Mak - er, thanks.

Chorus

Sing out with joy of heart! You too can have a part.

Live for the day when you'll say, "Life with - out end, at last!"

(See also Job 33:25; Ps. 72:7; Rev. 21:4.)

56

Please Hear My Prayer

(Psalm 54)

Heav-en-ly Fa-ther, please hear my song.
Thank you, Dear God, for grant-ing this day,
O how I long to do what is right!

You are my God; to you I be-long.
Giv-ing me life, and show-ing the way.
Help me, O Lord, to walk in the light.

Great is your name, be-yond all com-pare.
How I de-light in your ten-der care.
Give me the strength all bur-dens to bear.

Chorus

Gra-cious Je-ho-vah, please hear my prayer.

(See also Ex. 22:27; Ps. 106:4; Jas. 5:11.)

57 *The Meditation of My Heart*

(Psalm 19:14)

The med - i - ta - tion of my heart, The thoughts I pon - der through the
What - ev - er things are chaste and true, What - ev - er vir - tue there may

day— May they be pleas - ing to you, Lord, And keep me
be, What - ev - er things well - spo - ken of— May thoughts of

stead - fast in your way. When wor - ries weigh up - on my
these bring peace to me. How pre - cious are your thoughts, O

mind And make me rest - less in the night, Then
God! Be - yond all count - ing is their sum. So

The Meditation of My Heart

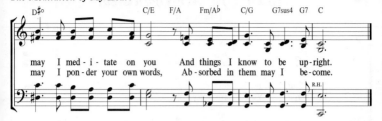

may I med-i-tate on you And things I know to be up-right.
may I pon-der your own words, Ab-sorbed in them may I be-come.

(See also Ps. 49:3; 63:6; 139:17, 23; Phil. 4:7, 8; 1 Tim. 4:15.)

58 *My Prayer of Dedication*

(Matthew 22:37)

Take my heart and may it love, Truth and
Take my feet and take my hands; Let them
Take my life and bring it, Lord, With your

wis-dom from a-bove. Take my mind, that
serve your wise com-mands. Take my voice and
will, in full ac-cord. Take my-self, may

I may serve Ful-ly, Lord, with-out re-serve.
let it sing Prais-es al-ways to my King.
all I do Be well-pleas-ing, Lord, to you.

(See also Ps. 40:8; John 8:29; 2 Cor. 10:5.)

59 *To God We Are Dedicated!*

(Matthew 16:24)

To Christ, by our God, Je-ho-vah, we have been
In prayer we have come be-fore Je-ho-vah to

drawn To be his dis-ci-ples from now on.
say We'll serve him for-ev-er and o-bey.

From Je-ho-vah's loft-y throne, Light of
It's a joy be-yond com-pare, One that

truth has bright-ly shone. In our hearts, our faith has
we most glad-ly share, As Je-ho-vah's name we

To God We Are Dedicated!

grown; Ourselves we a-gree to dis-own. To
bear, And news of his King-dom de-clare.

God we are ded-i-cat-ed; This is our choice. In

him and in Je-sus we now re-joice.

(See also Ps. 43:3; 107:22; John 6:44.)

60 *He Will Make You Strong*

(1 Peter 5:10)

There was a rea - son why God brought the truth to you And
God gave his own be - lov - ed Son in your be - half; On

called you from the dark-ness to the light. With-in your heart, he saw the
this ac-count, He wants you to suc - ceed. If He did not with-hold the

yearn-ing you then had To search for him and prac-tice what is right. You
gift of His dear Son, Then nev - er doubt He'll give the strength you need. He

prom-ised him in prayer to do his will; He helped you then, and he will help you
won't for - get the faith and love you've shown; He will not fail to care for all His

He Will Make You Strong

still.
own.
With Jesus' blood He bought you, to God you now belong. So
he will make you firm, and he will make you strong. He'll
guide you and protect you, as he has all along. Yes, he will make you firm,
and he will make you strong.

(See also Rom. 8:32; 14:8, 9; Heb. 6:10; 1 Pet. 2:9.)

What Sort of Person I Should Be

(2 Peter 3:11)

Lyrics:

How can I re-pay you, what gift can I give To thank you, Je-ho-vah, for the life that I live? I look in my heart with your Word as my mir-ror; The per-son I see, may you help me see clear-er. My life I have prom-ised in

Help me to ex-am-ine, and help me to see Just what sort of per-son you de-sire me to be. Those loy-al to you, you will loy-al-ly trea-sure; May I be a-mong those who bring your heart plea-sure. (End)

What Sort of Person I Should Be

ser - vice to you, But not from mere du - ty will I

do what I do. Whole - souled and whole - heart - ed I

serve you by choice; May I be one

more who makes you re - joice.

(See also Ps. 18:25; 116:12; 119:37; Prov. 11:20.)

62
To Whom Do We Belong?
(Romans 14:8)

To whom do you be-long? Which god do you now o-bey? Your
To whom do you be-long? Which god will you now o-bey? For
To whom do I be-long? Je-ho-vah I will o-bey. My

mas-ter is he to whom you bow. He is your god; you serve him now. You
one god is false and one is true, So make your choice; it's up to you. Shall
Fa-ther in heav-en I shall serve; I'll pay my vows with-out re-serve. He

can-not serve two gods; Both mas-ters can nev-er share The
Cae-sar of this world Pos-sess your al-le-giance still? Or
bought me at great cost; De-vot-ed to him I'll stay. The

love of your heart in its ev-'ry part. To nei-ther you would be fair.
will you o-bey the true God to-day By al-ways do-ing his will?
death of his Son my ran-som has won; His name I'll hon-or each day.

(See also Josh. 24:15; Ps. 116:14, 18; 2 Tim. 2:19.)

63

Ever Loyal

(Psalm 18:25)

Ev - er loy - al to Je - ho - vah, Loy - al love we wish to show.
Ev - er loy - al to our broth - ers, Stick - ing close in times of need.
Ev - er loy - al to their guid - ance When our broth - ers take the lead.

As a peo - ple, ded - i - cat - ed, His com - mands we want to know.
Ev - er car - ing, al - ways trust - ing, Ev - er kind in word and deed.
When they give us clear di - rec - tion, May our mind and heart give heed.

His ad - vice will nev - er fail us, And his coun - sel we o - bey.
We show hon - or to our broth - ers And re - spect them from the heart.
Then the bless - ing from Je - ho - vah Will be ours to make us strong.

He is loy - al; we can trust him. From his side we'll nev - er stray.
Let the Bi - ble draw us clos - er; From their side we'll nev - er part.
When we're loy - al, ev - er faith - ful, To Je - ho - vah we'll be - long.

(See also Ps. 149:1; 1 Tim. 2:8; Heb. 13:17.)

Make the Truth Your Own

(Proverbs 3:1, 2)

The way of the truth is the best way of
The ef - forts you make and the time you are
Com - pared with our God, we are all lit - tle

liv - ing, But no one can live your life
spend - ing In ser - vice to God and his
chil - dren And need his di - rec - tion and

for you. So heed the ad - vice that Je -
King - dom Will yield rich re - sults and a
coun - sel. So walk ev - 'ry day with our

ho - vah is giv - ing; Be - lieve what he
life that's un - end - ing, A life full of
Fa - ther in heav - en; Re - ceive his rich

Make the Truth Your Own

tells you is true.
good things to come. Make the truth your
bless - ing in full.

own. Make it live, yes, make it real.

And then feel the joy Je - ho - vah

gives you When you make the truth your own.

(See also Ps. 26:3; Prov. 8:35; 15:31; John 8:31, 32.)

65 "This Is the Way"

(Isaiah 30:20, 21)

"This Is the Way"

Way to life; This is the Way. Don't look a-

side; Not for a mo-ment stray! God's voice is call-ing: 'This is the

Way; Do not look back, for yes, This is the Way.'

(See also Ps. 32:8; 139:24; Prov. 6:23.)

66
Serving Jehovah Whole-Souled
(Matthew 22:37)

O Je-ho-vah, Sov-'reign Rul-er, You are the one I love and o-bey.
Fa-ther, all your works ex-alt you. Earth, moon, and stars your glo-ry pro-claim.

You de-serve my full de-vo-tion; Your trust in me I shall not be-tray.
I do give my life to serve you; With all my strength I'll make known your name.

Your com-mands I loy-al-ly fol-low; All you wish I glad-ly will do.
To my pledge of full ded-i-ca-tion, I will ev-er strive to be true.

Chorus

O Je-ho-vah, you are wor-thy; Whole-souled de-vo-tion I give to you.

(See also Deut. 6:15; Ps. 40:8; 113:1-3; Eccl. 5:4; John 4:34.)

67 *Pray to Jehovah Each Day*

(1 Thessalonians 5:17)

Pray to Je - ho - vah, the Hear - er of prayer. This is our
Pray to Je - ho - vah, give thanks that we live, Ask - ing for -
Pray to Je - ho - vah when trou - bles ap - pear. He is our

priv - 'lege, for his name we bear. O - pen your heart as you
give - ness as we do for - give. May we con - fess to our
Fa - ther and ev - er so near. Seek his pro - tec - tion, and

would to a friend, Trust that on Him you can al - ways de -
God whom we trust. He is our Mak - er and knows we are
look for his aid; Al - ways be trust - ing and nev - er a -

pend. Pray to Je - ho - vah each day.
dust. Pray to Je - ho - vah each day.
fraid. Pray to Je - ho - vah each day.

(See also Matt. 6:9-13; 26:41; Luke 18:1.)

68

A Prayer of the Lowly One

(Psalm 4:1)

Je - ho - vah God, I call to you and ask you: "Hear my prayer." My
Your Word has been my com - fort and a ref - uge when I'm weak, Ex -

wounds are deep and slow to heal; my load is hard to bear. De -
press - ing feel - ings dear to me in words I can - not speak. Please

spon - dent thoughts and dis - ap - point - ed hopes have left me weak. O
build in me the faith and trust that your Word does im - part. And

God of com - fort, care for me; your fa - vor I do seek.
help me al - ways know your love is great - er than my heart.

A Prayer of the Lowly One

Do raise me up; help me en-dure. When I'm in doubt, make my hope sure. From deep de-spair, I turn to you. Je-ho-vah God, my strength re-new.

(See also Ps. 42:6; 119:28; 2 Cor. 4:16; 1 John 3:20.)

69 *Make Me Know Your Ways*

(Psalm 25:4)

We're gath - ered to - geth - er Je - ho - vah, our God, Ac -
Un - reach - a - bly high is your wis - dom, O God; Your

cept - ing your warm in - vi - ta - tion. Your
judg - ments we find re - as - sur - ing. Your

Word is a lamp that lights up our road - way, The
Word is a source of un - end - ing won - der; Your

source of di - vine ed - u - ca - tion.
say - ings of truth are en - dur - ing.

Make Me Know Your Ways

Teach me your ways, and make me un-der-stand; In-cline my ear to hear your wise com-mand. Cause me to walk in ways of truth and right, And make your law my prin-ci-pal de-light.

(See also Ex. 33:13; Ps. 1:2; 119:27, 35, 73, 105.)

70 "Make Sure of the More Important Things"

(Philippians 1:10)

How great our need to-day for dis-cern-ment, To
And what could be of great-er im-por-tance Than
If we take care to do what's im-por-tant, Our

know the things that are true, To
shar-ing King-dom good news, To
faith will make us se-cure. We'll

know which things have great-er im-por-tance, To
find our Fa-ther's lost lit-tle sheep, And to
know the peace be-yond hu-man think-ing And

know which things we must do! Love what is
help them his way to choose? They need to
keep our hope ev-er sure. True friends we'll

"Make Sure of the More Important Things"

(See also Ps. 97:10; Matt. 22:37; John 21:15-17; Acts 10:42.)

71
God's Gift of Holy Spirit
(Luke 11:13)

Sov - 'reign, Je - ho - vah, mer - ci - ful Fa - ther,
Greater you are than our sin - ful hearts.
Light - en our bur - den, soft - en our an - guish,
Give us the com - fort your spir - it im - parts.

Fa - ther, we all fall short of your glo - ry;
Times there have been when we've lost our way.
God, we be - seech you: Please may you grant us
Your ho - ly spir - it to guide us each day.

When we are wea - ry, weak, or dis - cour - aged,
Your ac - tive force will our hearts re - new.
Give us the strength to mount up like ea - gles;
May we re - ceive ho - ly spir - it from you.

(See also Ps. 51:11; John 14:26; Acts 9:31.)

72 *Cultivating the Quality of Love*

(1 Corinthians 13:1-8)

We hum-bly bow to our God in prayer, That all his qual-i-ties we may share. But
It's not e-nough to use just the mind, As we keep teach-ing the sheep we find. We

most im-por-tant of all those things Is love, which hav-ing his spir-it brings. We
need to love them in word and deed, While help-ing them on His Word to feed. Love

may be tal-ent-ed, wise, or bold, But we are noth-ing if love grows cold. So
helps us pa-tient-ly suf-fer wrong, Bears heav-y loads when it's real-ly strong. And

may we cul-ti-vate last-ing love; Then we'll en-dure and please God a-bove.
so re-mem-ber in each tra-vail, Love bears all things; it will nev-er fail.

(See also John 21:17; 1 Cor. 13:13; Gal. 6:2.)

73. Love Intensely From the Heart

(1 Peter 1:22)

Love must come from deep in our hearts, There is the place af-fec-tion starts;
When our love is pure and in-tense, We will be slow to take of-fense;

Real fel-low feel-ing it im-parts For all our broth-ers dear.
Rea-son we have for con-fi-dence In all our broth-ers true.

We will find the way to ex-press Lov-ing in-ten-tions we pos-sess,
Loy-al friend-ships, we cul-ti-vate; Each oth-er we ap-pre-ci-ate.

Prac-tic-ing God's large heart-ed-ness, Prov-ing our love sin-cere.
Plea-sur-a-bly we con-gre-gate, Gain-ing our strength a-new.

Let us love in word and deed,
Day by day we all trans-gress;

Love Intensely From the Heart

Be - ing gen - er - ous to those in need, Let - ting good - ness
Thought - less words can of - ten cause dis - tress. So we must show

take the lead With each op - por - tu - ni - ty.
ten - der - ness To those whom our God does love.

Hon - or and re - spect we dis - play; Kind - ly con - cern will
True com - pan - ions we'll ev - er be, Strength - en - ing bonds with

be our way. Our broth - ers' faults we won't be - tray.
con - stan - cy. Let love be your i - den - ti - ty.

Ev - er loy - al we will be, Guard - ing pre - cious u - ni - ty.
Mag - ni - fy - ing God a - bove, Im - i - tate Je - ho - vah's love.

(See also 1 Pet. 2:17; 3:8; 4:8; 1 John 3:11.)

74

The Joy of Jehovah

(Nehemiah 8:10)

Signs of the times are her-ald-ing the King-dom. Good news we tell for
Look to our God, you lov-ers of Je-ho-vah. No need to fear, for

all to hear. Lift up your heads, and look to your sal-va-tion;
he is strong. Stand up and shout with voic-es loud as thun-der;

Time for de-liv-er-ance is near! The joy of Je-ho-vah is our
Sing to our God a joy-ous song!

strong-hold. Sing loud, and raise a joy-ful cry. Re-

The Joy of Jehovah

joice in the hope, and show a grate-ful heart, All give praise and laud our God on high. The joy of Je-ho-vah is our strong-hold. His name all men must come to know. With con-stant de-vo-tion to our God and King, God-ly joy in ser-vice we will show.

(See also 1 Chron. 16:27; Ps. 112:4; Luke 21:28; John 8:32.)

75

Our Reasons for Joy

(Matthew 5:12)

Our rea - sons for joy are a - bun - dant, Like rich - es in - creas - ing in
We glad - ly be - hold his pro - duc - tions, The heav - ens, the sea, and the

worth. De - sir - a - ble things of all na - tions Are join - ing us in all the
land. We gaze at the book of cre - a - tion, Ap - plaud - ing the work of his

earth. The joy in our heart is well - found - ed, With
hand. Tri - um - phant - ly we now bear wit - ness, Pro -

roots reach - ing deep in God's Word. We dai - ly par - take of its
claim - ing the King - dom of God. The news of its birth and its

teach - ings; Faith fol - lows the things we have heard. Our
bless - ings, We joy - ous - ly spread all a - broad. E -

Our Reasons for Joy

cau - es for joy are deep - seat - ed, Like em - bers that burn in our
ter - nal re - joic - ing ap - proach - es, Like day - light that fol - lows the

hearts. Though trou - bles and tri - als be - set us, En -
night. The prom - ised new earth and new heav - ens Will

dur - ance Je - ho - vah im - parts. Je - ho - vah our God is our
bring ev - er - las - ting de - light.

joy, The work of his hands our de - light. How deep are his

thoughts, how great are his works, A - bound - ing in good - ness and might!

(See also Deut. 16:15; Isa. 12:6; John 15:11.)

76
Jehovah, God of Peace
(Philippians 4:9)

Je - ho - vah, God of peace, God of love that will not cease.
This world seeks peace in vain. They have sown and reaped much pain.
Your spir - it aids our sight As your Word gives need - ed light.

Grant us peace - ful, calm con - di - tions, That good fruit - age may in - crease.
But up - on your fa - vored peo - ple, Peace de - scends like gen - tle rain.
We are guid - ed and pro - tect - ed In a world as dark as night.

Your coun - sel we have sought; With your Son our lives were bought.
As we dis - cern your will And our vows to you ful - fill,
May peace just like the dew Calm our thoughts, re - fresh us too,

May you grant us now your own peace That ex - cels all hu - man thought.
May you please now bless our ef - forts And more peace in us in - still.
That our hearts and men - tal pow - ers Might be safe by means of you.

(See also Ps. 4:8; Phil. 4:6, 7; 1 Thess. 5:23.)

77

Be Forgiving

(Psalm 86:5)

Lov - ing - ly Je - ho - vah Made pro - vi - sion through his Son
We re - ceive such mer - cy When we act like God a - bove
Mer - cy is a vir - tue That we all should cul - ti - vate.

For our sins to be for - giv - en And for death to be un - done.
And for - give each oth - er free - ly, Show - ing em - pa - thy and love.
It will keep us from re - sent - ment, From the bit - ter - ness of hate.

If we tru - ly are re - pen - tant, His for - give - ness we can claim
Put - ting up with one an - oth - er, Put - ting hurt - ful - ness a - way;
When we im - i - tate Je - ho - vah, Who is un - sur - passed in love,

On the ba - sis of Christ's ran - som, Ask - ing par - don in his name.
Show - ing hon - or to our broth - er, Show - ing love's sur - pass - ing way.
We will tru - ly be for - giv - ing; We will be like God a - bove.

(See also Matt. 6:12; Eph. 4:32; Col. 3:13.)

78
Long-Suffering
(Galatians 5:22)

Our Sov-'reign Lord, Je-ho-vah, Is zeal-ous for his ho-ly
Long-suf-fer-ing is need-ed To keep us on our god-ly

name. He fer-vent-ly de-si-res To
path. It lets our heart be tran-quil, Pro-

clear it from un-right-teous blame. Through man-y gen-er-
tects us from un-right-teous wrath. It finds the good in

a-tions, Great en-dur-ance he has shown; Long-
oth-ers, Al-ways hop-ing for the best. It

Long-Suffering

suf - fer - ing and pa - tient, Not wea - ry has he
lets us keep our bal - ance In times when we're dis -

grown. His will is that sal - va - tion All
tressed. A - long with oth - er vir - tues That

sorts of peo - ple might at - tain. Long - suf - fer - ing for -
ho - ly spir - it can be - stow, Long - suf - fer - ing will

bear - ance By God shall not have been in vain.
help us To im - i - tate the God we know.

(See also Ex. 34:14; Isa. 40:28; 1 Cor. 13:4, 7; 1 Tim. 2:4.)

79

The Power of Kindness

(Ephesians 4:32)

We're grate-ful to know Je-ho-vah, our God, For
Christ Je-sus in-vites the wea-ry at heart To
We see in our God and Je-sus our Lord, The

in his Word we find: Al-
leave their cares be-hind. How
per-sons we should be. In

though he is great in wis-dom and might, Je-
kind-ly his yoke, how light is his load, For
all that we do, we want to re-flect Their

ho-vah is lov-ing and kind.
he is re-fresh-ing and kind.
kind-ness and true em-pa-thy.

(See also Mic. 6:8; Matt. 11:28-30; Col. 3:12; 1 Pet. 2:3.)

80 *The Quality of Goodness*

(Psalm 119:66)

Know-ing good-ness from Je-ho-vah Is a joy through all our days. As our
In his like-ness he has made us So that we might cul-ti-vate All the
Those to whom we are re-lat-ed In the faith—our broth-er-hood— We will

Fa-ther in the heav-ens, He is good in all his ways. Show-ing
vir-tues he pos-sess-es And his good-ness im-i-tate. May we
show them spe-cial fa-vor, But to all may we do good. As we

fa-vor, grant-ing mer-cy, Far be-yond what we de-serve; He is
grow in god-ly good-ness, In his vir-tues may we share. Let us
share the King-dom good news And our hope with all we meet, May we

wor-thy of our wor-ship And the One we glad-ly serve.
pray for ho-ly spir-it, That its fruit-age we might bear.
al-ways be im-par-tial; May our good-ness be com-plete.

(See also Ps. 103:10; Mark 10:18; Gal. 5:22; Eph. 5:9.)

"Give Us More Faith"

(Luke 17:5)

Be-cause we are im-per-fect, O Je-ho-vah, The in-cli-
A-part from faith, no one can ful-ly please you. We must be-

na-tion of our heart is flawed. There is a
lieve our faith will be re-paid. And as a

sin that eas-i-ly en-snares us— A lack of
shield, our faith pro-vides a ref-uge. We face the

faith in you, the liv-ing God.
fu-ture firm and un-a-fraid.

Chorus

Give us more

"Give Us More Faith"

(See also Gen. 8:21; Heb. 11:6; 12:1.)

82 *Imitate Christ's Mildness*

(Matthew 11:28-30)

The great-est of men was our Lord Je-sus Christ; By
All you who are toil-ing with bur-den-some cares, He
'All you are just broth-ers,' our Lord Je-sus said. So

pride or am-bi-tion he was not en-ticed. God's
bids you come un-der the yoke that he bears. Re-
nev-er seek great-ness; serve oth-ers in-stead. The

pur-pose gave him the most prom-i-nent part; Yet,
fresh-ment you'll find as the King-dom you seek. Our
mild and the meek to our God have great worth; He

al-ways he proved him-self low-ly in heart.
Lord is mild-tem-pered; he fa-vors the meek.
prom-is-es they will in-her-it the earth.

(See also Matt. 5:5; 23:8; Prov. 3:34; Rom. 12:16.)

83

We Need Self-Control

(Romans 7:14-25)

We love Je-ho-vah with heart, mind, and soul; But
Sa-tan's temp-ta-tions con-front us each day, And
Each word and ac-tion re-flects on God's name, So

since we are sin-ful, we need self-con-trol.
sin's law with-in us can lead us a-stray.
we must en-deav-or to keep free from blame.

Mind-ing the flesh brings trou-ble and strife.
Pow-er of truth is great-er than sin.
In all we do, we make this our goal:

Mind-ing the spir-it means peace and life.
Thanks to Je-ho-vah, our minds can win.
Al-ways main-tain-ing our self-con-trol.

(See also 1 Cor. 9:25; Gal. 5:23; 2 Pet. 1:6.)

84

"I Want To"

(Luke 5:13)

Oh, what love God's Son for us showed
When he left his Father's abode
That with men he might live, God's truth he could give;
This truth from his lips ever flowed.

Oh, what help Jehovah God gave
When he sent the faithful wise slave,
With whom we serve with joy, Our powers employ,
That meek ones we might help to save.

"I Want To"

Great - ly he did com - fort man - kind, Healed
Those in need can eas - i - ly tell When

those who were sick, lame, and blind. To his
we love them ev - er so well. So if

roy - al com - mis - sion he proved true, And
wid - ows and or - phans should ask you, Then

lov - ing - ly said: "I want to."
read - i - ly say: "I want to."

(See also John 18:37; Eph. 3:19; Phil. 2:7.)

85 *A Full Reward From Jehovah*

(Matthew 19:29)

Je - ho - vah is faith - ful and ful - ly a - ware Of all those who serve him whole-
It   may be by choice or by their lot in life; There are some who sin - gle re -

souled.   He knows there are times their de - vo - tion and zeal   Re-
main.   By seek - ing the King - dom of God to the full,   In

sult in their loss as fore - told.   If   you have left hous - es or
god - ly de - vo - tion they gain.   By mak - ing the room for their

fam - 'ly or friends,   Be sure that our God knows the sum.   He
un - wed-ded state,   At   times they are lone - ly, we know.   As

A Full Reward From Jehovah

(See also Judg. 11:38-40; Ruth 2:12; Matt. 19:12.)

Faithful Women, Christian Sisters

(Romans 16:2)

Faithful Women, Christian Sisters

faithful women, ones we know by name.
fine examples all can imitate.
God's approval, may you never fear.

There were others favored by Jehovah,
Christian sisters, walking in their footsteps,
Christian sisters, may Jehovah keep you

Nameless in the record, their faith was just the same.
Worthy is your service and happy your estate.
Firm in your conviction, your prize is drawing near.

(See also Phil. 4:3; 1 Tim. 2:9, 10; 1 Pet. 3:4, 5.)

Now We Are One
(Genesis 2:23, 24)

This is at last bone of my bone, Flesh of my flesh; Now I'm not a-lone.

God has pro-vid-ed a part-ner, Some-one to call my own.

Now we are one; Now we can be All that Je-ho-vah made us to be.

As man and wom-an to-geth-er, We are a fam-i-ly.

Now We Are One

Ev-'ry day we'll serve our God a-bove. As he
shows the way, un-fail-ing love we'll dis-play. As we have vowed,
so may it be. Sea-sons of joy, may we come to see. Oh, may we hon-or Je-ho-vah,
And may you al-ways be my love.

(See also Gen. 29:18; Eccl. 4:9, 10; 1 Cor. 13:8.)

88 *Children Are a Trust From God*

(Psalm 127:3-5)

When a man be-comes a fa-ther And a wom-an has a child of her
All the words God has com-mand-ed— They must al-ways prove to be on your

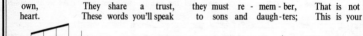

own, They share a trust, they must re-mem-ber, That is not
heart. These words you'll speak to sons and daugh-ters; This is your

theirs, not theirs a-lone. The gift they share is from Je-
trust, this is your part. To them you'll speak a-long your

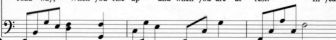

ho-vah; Of life and love he is the one true Source. To par-ents
road-way, When you rise up and when you are at rest. In years to

Children Are a Trust From God

he gives sure di - rec - tion That they may fol - low the wis - est
come, may they re - mem - ber, May they be faith - ful, may they be

Chorus

course.
blessed. A sa - cred trust you have been giv - en; A pre - cious

life is in your hands. You can be - stow the great - est

fa - vor; In - struct your child in God's com - mands.

(See also Deut. 6:6, 7; Eph. 6:4; 1 Tim. 4:16.)

89 Jehovah's Warm Appeal: "Be Wise, My Son"

(Proverbs 27:11)

Young man and young wom-an, do give your heart to
me. My foe who now taunts me will then be made to
see. Your youth and de-vo-tion to me you free-ly
give; You show all the world that for me you real-ly

Re-joice and take plea-sure in giv-ing me your
all, And though you may stum-ble, I'll raise you if you
fall. No mat-ter who fails you or proves to be un-
true, Take com-fort in know-ing I'll al-ways cher-ish

Jehovah's Warm Appeal: "Be Wise, My Son"

(See also Deut. 6:5; Eccl. 11:9; Isa. 41:13.)

90 *Beauty in Gray-Headedness*

(Proverbs 16:31)

Here with us are a - ged ones, Those whose youth has
Come - ly is gray-head - ed - ness Found in ways of

passed. Here a - mong us they en - dure;
right. Beau - ti - ful are faith - ful ones

Still they're hold - ing fast. Loss of strength be -
In Je - ho - vah's sight. May we al - ways

sets them all; Loss of mates for some.
rec - og - nize They were once young too.

Beauty in Gray-Headedness

Father, please confirm their faith In the life to come.
Loyally they gave their best When their strength was new.

Chorus

Father, you remember How in faith they've run. Give them your assurance; May they hear, "Well done!"

(See also Matt. 25:21, 23; Ps. 71:9, 18; Prov. 20:29; Luke 22:28; 1 Tim. 5:1.)

91 *My Father, My God and Friend*

(Hebrews 6:10)

Life in this world can be hard. Life in this world can bring
Gone are the days of my youth; Days of ca- lam- i- ty

tears and pain. Still ev- 'ry day I will say, "My
now are here. Still through the eyes of my faith, My

life is not in vain." For God is not un-
hope is bright and clear.

Chorus

righ- teous, And he re- mem- bers the love I've shown. So

My Father, My God and Friend

he is ev-er near me; With Je-ho-vah, I'm not a-lone. Yes, God is my pro-vid-er and my pro-tec-tor down to the end. Yes, Je-ho-vah is my Fa-ther, My God and Friend.

(See also Ps. 71:17, 18.)

"Preach the Word"

(2 Timothy 4:2)

God has com-mand-ed us this day; He has
Sea - sons of trou-ble we will face; Op-po-
Sea - sons of fa-vor we will see, And the

giv - en us a charge to o - bey. At
si - tion may bring shame and dis - grace. Though
need for us to teach, there will be. The

all times, be read - y to im - part The
preach - ing may out of sea - son seem, Our
way to sal - va - tion we pro - claim And

rea - son for the hope with - in your heart.
trust is in our God, who is su - preme.
help to sanc - ti - fy Je - ho - vah's name. So preach the

Chorus

"Preach the Word"

(See also Matt. 10:7; 24:14; Acts 10:42; 1 Pet. 3:15.)

93

"Let Your Light Shine"

(Matthew 5:16)

Je - sus has com - mand - ed That we shine our light,
With God's King - dom mes - sage Light on hearts is shed,
Light from fine works gleam - ing, Bright - ens up this world,

Like the sun, im - par - tial, That all might gain sight.
Com - fort brought to mourn - ers, Hope for those now dead.
To our words adds lus - ter, Like a price - less pearl.

Through God's Ho - ly Scrip - tures, Words of wis - dom shine.
Light from Scrip - ture guides us As we do His will;
May our light keep shin - ing As we do what's right,

May we now re - flect his light By our deeds so fine.
Gra - cious words, well - sea - soned too, Make it bright - er still.
Then our works will al - ways be Pleas - ing in God's sight.

(See also Ps. 119:130; Matt. 5:14, 15, 45; Col. 4:6.)

94 *Content With God's Good Gifts*
(James 1:17)

All per-fect pres-ents, each good gift, The things we're fond-est of,
We have no cause for anx-ious care Con-cern-ing dai-ly needs;
The loft-y things in hu-man eyes, To God are mere-ly vain.

The tru-ly wor-thy things in life, Come down from God a-bove.
We know the lov-ing care by him Who birds of heav-en feeds.
Let's use the days we're grant-ed now For things of last-ing gain.

With him there is no wa-ver-ing, No change, how-ev-er slight.
We give no place to worth-less things, No years to hurt-ful strife.
The rich-es that we store with God Are safe, though we may die.

Je-ho-vah is our Grand Pro-vid-er, The Source of life and light.
But sat-is-fied with God's pro-vi-sions, We lead a sim-ple life.
We prize the gift of true con-tent-ment And keep a sim-ple eye.

(See also Jer. 45:5; Matt. 6:25-34; 1 Tim. 6:8; Heb. 13:5.)

95 *"Taste and See That Jehovah Is Good"*

(Psalm 34:8)

Our ser - vice to God we cher - ish; We
For those in the full - time ser - vice, Rich

val - ue our priv - 'lege to preach. We
bles - sings and trea - sures a - bound. By

buy out the time and give God our best, For
trust - ing in God to care for their needs, In

ma - ny we still need to reach.
all things con - tent - ment is found.

"Taste and See That Jehovah Is Good"

God's Word invites us: 'Come taste and see—
See that Jehovah is good.'
Godly devotion brings greatest gain,
We know we've done all we could.

(See also Mark 14:8; Luke 21:2; 1 Tim. 1:12; 6:6.)

96 *Seek Out Deserving Ones*

(Matthew 10:11-15)

In preach - ing the King - dom, our Lord showed the way, In -
All those who re - ceive you re - ceive him as well. Their

struct - ing us how to pro - ceed: 'Wher -
heart God will o - pen up wide. Their

ev - er you go, seek in ear - nest to find Those a -
right dis - po - si - tion for un - end - ing life Will im -

ware of their spir - i - tual need. By
pel them to serve at your side. And

Seek Out Deserving Ones

greet - ing the house - hold and wish - ing it peace, To de -
nev - er be anx - ious a - bout what to say, For Je -

serv - ing ones peace you'll im - part. If
ho - vah will help you to speak. Your

oth - ers should spurn you or turn you a - way, Shake the
an - swer when gra - cious and sea - soned with salt Will ap -

dust from your feet and de - part.'
peal to the hum - ble and meek.

(See also Acts 13:48; 16:14; Col. 4:6.)

97 *Forward, You Ministers of the Kingdom!*

(2 Timothy 4:5)

Go for-ward in preach-ing the King-dom To peo-ple in ev-'ry land. With love in your hearts for your neigh-bor, Help meek ones to take their stand. Our ser-vice to God is a priv-'lege; His word we are glad to pro-claim. Go

True min-is-ters keep press-ing for-ward With God's prize of life in view. We fol-low the steps of our Mas-ter With hearts that have been made new. The good news of God's com-ing King-dom Is some-thing that all need to hear. We

To-geth-er we press ev-er for-ward, God's rem-nant and oth-er sheep. The old and the young men and wom-en In step with the truth do keep. Our ser-vice we hold to be sa-cred; Our wor-ship is nev-er rou-tine. To

Forward, You Ministers of the Kingdom!

out in the field and keep preach - ing; Give
preach in the strength of Je - ho - vah; With
God may we prove ev - er wor - thy By

wit - ness to God's ho - ly name.
him there is noth - ing to fear! For - ward,
con - duct that's ho - ly and clean.

bold - ly preach the King - dom mes - sage ev - er far and wide.

For - ward, faith - ful, loy - al - ly re - main - ing on Je - ho - vah's side.

(See also Ps. 23:4; Acts 4:29, 31; 1 Pet. 2:21.)

Sowing Kingdom Seed
(Matthew 13:4-8)

Oh, come all you slaves of Je - ho - vah,
Some seed that you sow will be scat - tered
How much of your work is suc - cess - ful

Who've giv - en your heart and your soul.
On hearts as re - sis - tant as stone.
May of - ten de - pend much on you.

Come out to the work of our Mas - ter,
Though these may re - spond for a sea - son,
With pa - tience and love for your neigh - bors,

And learn from his steps and his role.
The want of their hearts will be known.
Their hearts may be o - pened a - new.

Sowing Kingdom Seed

The seed of the truth, you sow with-out fear
When thorns choke the word, then greed fills their hearts;
By be - ing a - lert you'll ward off their fears,

On hearts that are a - ble to yield
The things of the world they pre - fer.
With mea - sures some gen - tle some bold.

Fine fruit to God's praise as you faith - ful - ly work,
Yet, some seed may pros - per; you will see re - sults
And thus with re - joic - ing you can hope to reap

And you do your full share in the field.
From the ground that is good, fine, and pure.
At least thir - ty if not hun - dred - fold.

(See also Matt. 13:19-23; 22:37.)

99 *Praising Earth's New King*

(Revelation 7:9)

A mul-ti-tude is gath-er-ing from ev-'ry tribe and na-tion, Col-lect-ed by the Christ and his a-noint-ed con-gre-ga-tion. God's King-dom has been brought to birth; His will shall soon be done on earth. This

We hail the Christ, our reign-ing King, with sounds of ju-bi-la-tion. This Prince of Peace shall do God's will and bring a-bout sal-va-tion. We see the joys that lie a-head: An earth re-leased from fear and dread, The

Praising Earth's New King

hope is a gift of price-less worth, giv-ing joy and con-so-
grand res-ur-rec-tion of the dead. What a time for ex-ul-

la - tion.
ta - tion!

Chorus

Praise our God, Je - ho - vah; Praise his Son, Christ Je - sus,

Who through the ran-som have set us free. Now we have the hope to

live on the earth And serve God e - ter - nal - ly.

(See also Ps. 2:6; 45:1; Isa. 9:6; John 6:40.)

100

We Are Jehovah's Army!

(Joel 2:7)

We are Je-ho-vah's ar-my, Freed from Sa-tan's chains, Preach-ing a-bout God's King-dom, In which Je-sus now reigns. As we press on faith-ful-ly, Each a vol-un-teer,

We are Je-ho-vah's ser-vants, Search-ing for his sheep, Those who are lost and lone-ly, Those who sigh and who weep. These we try to find and feed With re-peat-ed calls;

This is Je-ho-vah's ar-my Un-der Christ's com-mand, Ful-ly e-quipped for bat-tle, Each one firm-ly will stand. Cau-tious though we need to be, Up-right we re-main.

We Are Jehovah's Army!

(See also Eph. 6:11, 14; Phil. 1:7; Philem. 2.)

101 *Making Known the Kingdom Truth*

(Acts 20:20, 21)

There was a time we did not know The way a Chris - tian ought to go. Then Je - ho - vah sent the light, His King - dom truth so clear and bright. Our Fa - ther's will we then could see To serve the grand The - oc - ra - cy, To de - clare Je - ho - vah's fame, And help to glo - ri - fy his ho - ly name. We wit - ness now to all we

Making Known the Kingdom Truth

meet, From door to door and on the street. We take the time to help them see; We teach the truth that sets men free. And as we strive in ev-'ry land Je-ho-vah's wor-ship to ex-pand, May we serve our God as one Un-til Je-ho-vah says the work is done.

(See also Josh. 9:9; Isa. 24:15; John 8:12, 32.)

102
Join in the Kingdom Song!
(Psalm 98:1)

This is a song,   a hap-py song of vic-t'ry;
With this new song,   we ad-ver-tise the King-dom.
This King-dom song,   all hum-ble ones can mas-ter.

It mag-ni-fies   the One who is su-preme.
Christ Je-sus rules;   the earth is his do-main.
The words are clear,   their mes-sage warm and bright.

The words give hope   and prompt all to be loy-al.
And as fore-told,   there is a new-born na-tion;
In all the earth,   vast mul-ti-tudes have learned it,

Come sing with us;   en-joy its King-dom theme:
The King-dom heirs,   who wel-come Je-sus' reign: 'Come
And they in turn   still oth-ers now in-vite:

Chorus

Join in the Kingdom Song!

(See also Ps. 95:6; 1 Pet. 2:9, 10; Rev. 12:10.)

103

"From House to House"

(Acts 20:20)

From house to house, from door to door, Je-ho-vah's word we spread.
From house to house, from door to door, Sal-va-tion we pro-claim.
So let us go from door to door To spread the King-dom news.

From town to town, from farm to farm, Je-ho-vah's sheep are fed.
It comes to those who choose to call Up-on Je-ho-vah's name.
And wheth-er it's em-braced or not, We'll let the peo-ple choose.

This good news that God's King-dom rules, As Je-sus Christ fore-told,
But how can they call on the name Of One they do not know?
At least we'll name Je-ho-vah's name, His glo-rious truth de-clare.

Is be-ing preached through-out the earth By Chris-tians young and old.
So to their hous-es and their doors, The sa-cred name must go.
And as we go from door to door, We'll find his sheep are there.

(See also Acts 2:21; Rom. 10:14.)

104

Praise Jah With Me

(Psalm 146:2)

Praise Jah with me; Loud let it ring!
He gives us life, breath, and ev'ry good thing.
Each day and night, His name we bless.
His perfect love clothes His almightiness.
We sing his praise, and his name we confess.

Praise Jah with me. He satisfies
And hears our prayers as our needs he supplies.
His mighty arm Strengthens the weak;
His holy spirit sustains all the meek.
His name we praise; Of his power we speak.

Praise Jah with me. Our God is just;
He brings all comfort, in him we can trust.
Wrongs he will right; Hearts he will heal.
Rich Kingdom blessings all mankind will feel.
Come let us praise him with joy and with zeal!

(See also Ps. 94:18, 19; 145:21; 147:1; 150:2.)

105 *The Heavens Declare God's Glory*

(Psalm 19)

The heav- ens tell the glo- ry of Je- ho- vah.
Je- ho- vah's law is per- fect, life- re- stor- ing,
The fear of God is pure and stands for- ev- er.

The work of his own hand in skies a- bove we see.
And his re- mind- ers guide the steps of old and young.
The worth of his com- mands ex- ceeds the fin- est gold.

And each new day brings to him right- ful praise.
His rul- ings prove to be true, right, and just.
His or- ders lead and pre- serve all his own.

The star- lit night pro- claims his might And his true maj- es- ty.
His word is sure, his law so pure, So sweet up- on the tongue.
His hon- or, fame, and ho- ly name, We loy- al- ly up- hold.

(See also Ps. 111:9; 145:5; Rev. 4:11.)

106 *Gaining Jehovah's Friendship*

(Psalm 15)

Who is your friend, O God? Who in your tent may dwell?
Who is your friend, O God? Who may ap-proach your throne?
Roll-ing our cares on you, Bar-ing our hearts in prayer,

Who gains your friend-ship? Who gains your trust? Who real-ly knows you well?
Who brings de-light and Makes you re-joice? Whose name to you is known?
Draw-ing us clos-er, Bond-ing in love, Feel-ing your dai-ly care,

All who em-brace your Word, All who have faith in you,
All who ex-alt your name, All who your Word o-bey,
We yearn to be your friend. Long may our friend-ship grow.

All who are loy-al, all who are just, Liv-ing the truth for you.
All who are faith-ful, hon-est in heart, Truth-ful in all they say.
No great-er Friend could we ev-er gain, No great-er Friend we'll know.

(See also Ps. 139:1; 1 Pet. 5:6, 7.)

107 *Come to Jehovah's Mountain*

(Isaiah 2:2-4)

Raise your eyes and be-hold, Far a-bove the high-est hill.
Je - sus gave the com-mand To go forth and preach the word.

There stands Je-ho-vah's moun-tain Lift-ed up in this day.
Good news a-bout the King-dom Reach-es all men to-day.

Peo - ple come from a-far, Ev-'ry-where from sea to sea,
Christ now rules from on high, Urg-ing all to take his side.

Call - ing to one an-oth-er, 'Come serve God and o-bey.' Now the
Meek ones who hear his voice Let God's Word show them the way. What a

Come to Jehovah's Mountain

time has ar-rived For the small, a great na-tion to be. As we
joy to be-hold How a great crowd con-tin-ues to grow! Yes, we

grow and we thrive, God's di-rec-tion and bless-ing we see.
all have a share, Help-ing oth-ers Je-ho-vah to know.

Mil - lions now come to God And ac-cept his sov-'reign-ty.
Let us lift up the voice, Call-ing out for all to hear,

Loy - al they vow to be And from his side nev-er stray.
'Come to Je-ho-vah's moun-tain, Here for-ev-er to stay.'

(See also Ps. 43:3; 99:9; Isa. 60:22; Acts 16:5.)

108 *Praise Jehovah for His Kingdom*

(Revelation 21:2)

Je-ho-vah a-noint-ed his Son To rule o-ver ev-'ry-
one. His throne is es-tab-lished on jus-tice, That
God's will on earth may be done.

Christ's broth-ers are cho-sen and called. God gives them their own new
birth. This bride class will share in the King-dom And
bring Par-a-dise to this earth.

Chorus

Praise Jah for his ho-ly A-noint-ed. Hail Je-sus, O you faith-ful sheep, Who

Praise Jehovah for His Kingdom

loy - al - ly fol - low day af - ter day and all his com - mand - ments keep. Praise Jah for his ho - ly A - noint - ed, the Rul - er of heav - en - ly fame, A - noint - ed with ex - ul - ta - tion and might To hon - or God's ho - ly name.

(See also Prov. 29:4; Isa. 66:7, 8; John 10:4; Rev. 5:9, 10.)

109 *Hail Jehovah's Firstborn!*

(Hebrews 1:6)

Hail Je-ho-vah's First-born, God's du-ly ap-point-ed
Hail Je-ho-vah's First-born, Who died so that we may

King. He reigns for truth and jus-tice; Rich
live. He hum-bly paid the ran-som; Our

bless-ings his rule will bring. With dig-ni-ty and
sins God can now for-give. The bride of Christ a-

splen-dor And love for God's great name, He'll
waits him, A-dorned for him in white. This

Hail Jehovah's Firstborn!

vin - di - cate Je - ho - vah, His sov - 'reign - ty pro -
mar - riage in the heav - ens Will prove God's rule is

claim.
right.

Chorus

Hail Je - ho - vah's First - born! All
praise God's a - noint - ed Son. In - stalled up - on Mount
Zi - on, His King - ship has now be - gun!

(See also Ps. 2:6; 45:3, 4; Rev. 19:8.)

God's Wondrous Works

(Psalm 139)

O God, you know my rest and wak-ing, When I lie down and when I rise a-new. You search my thought, my in-most in-cli-na-tion, The words I speak, the ways I walk, you know them too. You saw when I was made in se-cret, My ve-ry bones not hid-den from your sight. You saw my form; its parts were down in writ-ing. I praise the won-der of your ways, ex-tol your

God's Wondrous Works

might. Your knowl-edge, God, is won-drous, fear-in-spir-ing; Of this my soul is ve-ry well a-ware. If I should fear that dark-ness might en-fold me, Your spir-it, God, would find me, e-ven there. Where could I hide from you, Je-ho-vah, Or be con-cealed, be hid-den from your face? Not in the heights nor in the depth of She-ol, Not in the dark nor in the sea, there is no place.

(See also Ps. 66:3; 94:19; Jer. 17:10.)

111

He Will Call

(Job 14:13-15)

Life, like a mist, ap-pears for just a day, Then dis-ap-pears to-mor-row.
Friends of our God, though they may pass a-way, Will nev-er be for-sak-en.

All that we are can quick-ly fade a-way, Re-placed with tears and sor-row.
All those a-sleep who in God's mem-'ry stay, From death he will a-wak-en.

If a man should die, can he live a-gain? Hear the prom-ise God has
Then we'll come to see all that life can be: Par-a-dise e-ter-nal-

made:
ly.

He will call; The dead will an-swer. They shall

He Will Call

live at his com-mand. For he will have a long-ing For the
work of his own hand. So have faith, and do not won-der, For our
God can make us stand. And we shall live for-
ev-er, As the work of his own hand.

(See also John 6:40; 11:11, 43; Jas. 4:14.)

112

Great God, Jehovah

(Exodus 34:6, 7)

Great God, Je-ho-vah, you are de-serv-ing,
Par-don-ing er-ror, sin, and trans-gres-sion,
Let men and an-gels join in your prais-es;

Wor-thy of the high-est praise, Good and just in all your ways.
Mer-ci-ful to those like you, Those who prac-tice mer-cy too.
Let your name be sanc-ti-fied, Nev-er more to be de-nied.

Your throne is found-ed firm-ly on jus-tice;
Your king-ly jus-tice, your lov-ing-kind-ness,
Soon may your King-dom, rul-ing in heav-en,

You are God to end-less days.
You have shown in all you do.
Make your will be done earth wide.

(See also Deut. 32:4; Prov. 16:12; Matt. 6:10; Rev. 4:11.)

113 *Grateful for God's Word*

(Philippians 2:16)

Je-ho-vah, our Fa-ther, we want to ex-press
En-dowed are its pag-es with hu-man ap-peal.
Your word has such pow-er to reach deep in-side,

How grate-ful we are that your Word we pos-sess!
Your proph-ets were like us; they felt what we feel.
Yes, e-ven the spir-it and soul to di-vide.

Its writ-ers you in-spir-ed to tell your ver-y thought.
We gath-er faith and cour-age by learn-ing of their lives.
It search-es our in-ten-tions and mo-tives of our hearts.

By Scrip-ture we're guid-ed; by you we are taught.
Our heart it re-fresh-es; our soul it re-vives.
It of-fers cor-rec-tion and wis-dom im-parts.

(See also Ps. 119:16, 162; 2 Tim. 3:16; Jas. 5:17; 2 Pet. 1:21.)

114 *God's Own Book—A Treasure*

(Proverbs 2:1)

There is a book that by its man - y pag - es,
They wrote a rec - ord true of God's cre - a - tions,
To - day we live in times of joy un - bound - ed.

Brings peace and joy and hope to hu - man - kind.
How by his might this u - ni - verse ap - peared.
God's King - dom now is here with Christ as Lord.

Its won - drous thoughts are charged with such great pow - er;
They al - so told how man at first was sin - less
This is the day Je - ho - vah grants sal - va - tion

It brings life to the "dead," sight to the "blind."
But how his Par - a - dise then dis - ap - peared.
To all who come to him in full ac - cord.

God's Own Book—A Treasure

That pre-cious book is God's own Ho-ly Bi-ble.
They fur-ther told a-bout a cer-tain an-gel
With-in his book are found these cheer-ful tid-ings;

Its words were penned by men whom God in-spired,
Who chal-lenged God and spurned his sov-'reign-ty.
A sa-cred ban-quet feast on which to feed.

By men who tru-ly loved their God Je-ho-vah,
That chal-lenge led to sin and man's great sor-row,
It of-fers peace be-yond all hu-man think-ing;

And by his ho-ly spir-it they were fired.
But soon will come Je-ho-vah's vic-to-ry.
This Liv-ing Trea-sure beck-ons all to read.

(See also 2 Tim. 3:16; 2 Pet. 1:21.)

115 *Making Our Way Successful*

(Joshua 1:8)

We delight in Jehovah's Word. May we
read it each day. Sound each thought in an
undertone; Meditate and obey.
May it guide ev'ry step we take,

When the kings ruled in Israel, They re-
ceived this command: 'Ev'ry king for him-
self must write God's Law in his own hand.
He must read in it all his days,

As we feed on God's Word each day, Hope and
comfort we find. Calm descends on our
troubled hearts; Faith in Him is refined.
When we truly embrace his Word,

Making Our Way Successful

Ev-'ry thought we ex-press.
That he may not trans-gress.'
We ma-ture and prog-ress.

Chorus

Read and med-i-tate, then o-bey. This Je-ho-vah will bless. Walk with him each and ev-'ry day. Find the way to suc-cess.

(See also Deut. 17:18; 1 Ki. 2:3, 4; Ps. 119:1; Jer. 7:23.)

116 *The Light Gets Brighter*

(Proverbs 4:18)

The proph - ets of old sought to learn of the Christ, The
Our Lord has ap - point - ed a trust - wor - thy slave, The

hope of all groan - ing cre - a - tion. God's spir - it re - vealed that Mes -
whom He gives food in due sea - son. The light of the truth has grown

si - ah would come, Pro - vid - ing the means of sal - va - tion. The
bright - er with time, Ap - peal - ing to heart and to rea - son. Our

time has ar - rived, the Mes - si - ah now reigns, The proof of his pres - ence is
path ev - er clear - er, our steps ev - er firm, We walk in the bright - ness of

The Light Gets Brighter

clear. How great is the fa-vor of learn-ing such things; In-to
day. All thanks to Je-ho-vah, the Source of all truth, We most

these e-ven an-gels would peer!
grate-ful-ly walk in his way.

Chorus

Our path now be-comes ev-er
bright-er; We walk in the full light of day. Be-

hold what our God is re-veal-ing; He guides us each step of the way.

(See also Rom. 8:22; 1 Cor. 2:10; 1 Pet. 1:12.)

117

We Must Be Taught

(Isaiah 50:4; 54:13)

Come with re - joic - ing, and learn a - bout Je - ho - vah.
Nev - er for - sak - ing our gath - er - ing to - geth - er,
Lips that sing praise, how en - cour - ag - ing to hear them!

"Come drink life's wa - ter," the spir - it has said.
We must be taught; we must learn what is right.
Tongues of the taught ones, how sweet is their sound!

Health - ful in - struc - tion, God has pro - vid - ed.
Here with God's spir - it, here with our broth - ers,
Oh, may we al - ways meet with God's peo - ple!

All those who hun - ger for truth will be fed.
Here we are strength - ened to walk in the light.
Oh, may we al - ways a - mong them be found!

(See also Heb. 10:24, 25; Rev. 22:17.)

118 *Welcome One Another*

(Romans 15:7)

Wel - come to all who gath - er here this day, To
Thanks to our God for broth - ers such as these, Who
God's in - vi - ta - tion reach - es all man - kind, That

hear God's Word and to learn his way.
wel - come us and who seek to please.
all sin - cere ones the truth may find.

Life - giv - ing truth he of - fers to us all; With
May we keep hold - ing men of that sort dear, And
God by his Son has drawn us to His side. So

thank - ful - ness of heart, we re - spond to his call.
now we wel - come oth - ers who meet with us here.
wel - come one an - oth - er with hearts o - pened wide.

(See also John 6:44; Phil. 2:29; Rev. 22:17.)

119

Come! Be Refreshed

(Hebrews 10:24, 25)

Come! Be Refreshed

move us with words that in-cite to fine deeds, They give us the strength to go
lov-ing sup-port from our fam-'ly of faith, We know that we're nev-er a-

on. We'll nev-er for-sake what Je-ho-vah com-mands; His
lone. So as we look for-ward to much bet-ter times, We'll

will is what we want to do. Our meet-ings in-struct us in
meet with the ones whom we love. And here at these meet-ings we'll

ways that are right; Our love for the truth they re-new.
learn how to live With wis-dom that comes from a-bove.

(See also Ps. 37:18; 140:1; Prov. 18:1; Eph. 5:16; Jas. 3:17.)

120 *Listen, Obey, and Be Blessed*
(Luke 11:28)

If we have lis - tened to Christ, will we show it? His teach - ing
Our way of life, like a house, gives pro - tec - tion When it is
Just as a tree root - ed deep by the wa - ters Gives of its

shines as it shows us the way. It makes us
built on the rock, not on sand. If we ap -
fruit when each sea - son ar - rives, If we o -

hap - py to hear and to know it, But we'll be
ply Je - sus' lov - ing di - rec - tion, We'll build a
bey as God's own sons and daugh - ters, We'll all be

blessed if we know and o - bey.
life which on bed - rock will stand.
blessed and en - joy end - less lives.

Listen, Obey, and Be Blessed

Chorus

Listen, obey, and be blessed
When you hear God's will expressed.
If you'd be happy and enter his rest,
Listen, obey, and be blessed.

(See also Deut. 28:2; Ps. 1:3; Prov. 10:22; Matt. 7:24-27.)

121
Encourage One Another
(Hebrews 10:24, 25)

As we en-cour-age one an-oth-er To
A word when spo-ken at the right time Is,
As we with eyes of faith are see-ing The

serve Je-ho-vah faith-ful-ly, We
oh, how com-fort-ing to hear! We
near-ness of Je-ho-vah's day, We

find the bonds of love are strength-ened; Fine
hear these words of con-so-la-tion From
need our gath-er-ing to-geth-er To

works bring peace and u-ni-ty. The
friends so faith-ful and so dear. How
keep us walk-ing in the way. U-

Encourage One Another

love we find a- mong God's peo - ple Gives
good it is to work to- geth - er With
nit - ed with Je- ho- vah's peo - ple, We

each the cour- age to en - dure. Our
those whose hopes and goals we share! We
hope to serve e - ter- nal - ly. So

con - gre- ga- tion is a ref - uge, A
seek to strength-en one an- oth - er And
we en- cour-age one an- oth - er To

place where we can feel se - cure.
help each one his bur - den bear.
hold to our in - teg- ri - ty.

(See also Luke 22:32; Acts 14:21, 22; Gal. 6:2; 1 Thess. 5:14.)

122

Myriads of Brothers

(Revelation 7:9, 10)

Myr - iads on myr - iads of broth - ers, Mil - lions for all to see,
Myr - iads on myr - iads of broth - ers, We preach both far and near
Myr - iads on myr - iads of broth - ers, God keeps us in his sight,

Each one a faith - ful wit - ness, Firm in in - teg - ri - ty.
"Good news of some - thing bet - ter," Which mil - lions long to hear.
Safe in his earth - ly court - yards, Serv - ing him day and night.

Myr - iads we are on myr - iads, Grow - ing, a might - y crowd,
And as we keep on preach - ing, Though we at times are stressed,
Myr - iads we are on myr - iads, With King - dom news we go,

From ev - 'ry na - tion and tribe and tongue, We praise our God a - loud.
Je - sus re - fresh - es the wea - ry souls; He gives us peace and rest.
God's fel - low work - ers we have be - come, Serv - ing him here be - low.

(See also Isa. 52:7; Matt. 11:29; Rev. 7:15.)

123 *Shepherds—Gifts in Men*

(Ephesians 4:8)

Help in our lives, Je - ho - vah pro - vides, Shep - herds to tend his flock.
Shep - herds who love us care how we feel; Gent - ly they guide the way.
God - ly ad - vice and coun - sel they give, That we may nev - er stray.

By their ex - am - ple they serve as guides, Show - ing us how to walk.
When we are hurt, they help us to heal, Kind in the words they say.
Thus they as - sist us, God's way to live, Serv - ing him ev - 'ry day.

Chorus

God gives us men who have earned our trust, Men who are loy - al and true.

They show con - cern for his pre - cious flock; Love them for all that they do.

(See also Isa. 32:1, 2; Jer. 3:15; John 21:15-17; Acts 20:28.)

124 Receive Them With Hospitality

(Acts 17:7)

Jeho-vah shows sincere hospitality. He
We never know the good that may come about When

cares for all without partiali-ty. He
we see those in need and we help them out. Though

gives both rain and sun, with-holding these from none; He
strang-ers they may be, in hospitali-ty, We

fills our hearts with food and good cheer. When-
lend a hand to care for their needs. Like

Receive Them With Hospitality

ev - er we show fa - vor to low - ly ones, We
Lyd - i - a of old, we say: 'Be my guest.' When

im - i - tate our God as be - lov - ed sons. Our
they come to our home, they find peace and rest. Our

Fa - ther will re - pay the good - ness we dis - play, Our
Fa - ther is a - ware of all those ev - 'ry - where, Who

kind - ness that is tru - ly sin - cere.
im - i - tate his mer - ci - ful deeds.

(See also Acts 16:14, 15; Rom. 12:13; 1 Tim. 3:2; Heb. 13:2; 1 Pet. 4:9.)

125 *Loyally Submitting to Theocratic Order*

(1 Corinthians 14:33)

As Je-ho-vah's peo-ple sound through-out the earth
God pro-vides his stew-ard and his ac-tive force.

Truths a-bout the King-dom and its price-less worth,
These will ev-er guide us in our Chris-tian course.

The-o-crat-ic or-der they must all o-bey
So may we be stead-fast, seek-ing God to please,

And re-main u-nit-ed, loy-al-ty dis-play.
Loy-al-ly pro-claim-ing all his wise de-crees!

Loyally Submitting to Theocratic Order

Chorus

Loy - al sub - mis - sion in rec - og - ni - tion,

This to our God we owe.

He gives pro - tec - tion, ten - der af - fec - tion,

Loy - al - ty to him we show.

(See also Luke 12:42; Heb. 13:7, 17.)

126 *Our Labor of Love*

(Psalm 127:1)

Our Labor of Love

build - ing stands, by our hands, As the proof there-of.
add - ed fame to your name; What a grand re - ward!

Chorus

Je-ho-vah God, it was a priv-'lege For us to build this place for you. May we con - tin - ue in your ser - vice through-out our days And bring you praise in all we do.

(See also Ps. 116:1; 147:1; Rom. 15:6.)

127 *A Place Bearing Your Name*

(1 Chronicles 29:16)

How great is the hon - or, Je - ho - vah, To build you a place for your
And now may we hon - or you, Fa - ther, By fill - ing this place with your

name! We of - fer it now with re - joic - ing To
praise. May glo - ry as - cend with the in - crease Of

add to your glo - ry and fame. What - ev - er the things we may
those who are learn - ing your ways. Com - mit - ting this place to your

give you, They right - ly were yours from the start. Our
wor - ship, We give it our gen - er - ous care. And

A Place Bearing Your Name

la - bor, our skill, our pos - ses - sions, We joy - ful - ly give from the
long may it stand as a wit - ness, Sup - port - ing the mes - sage we

Chorus

heart.
bear.
May we pre - sent this place to you, And

here may your name be known. We ded - i - cate this place to

you; Please ac - cept it as your own.

(See also 1 Ki. 8:18, 27; 1 Chron. 29:11-14; Acts 20:24.)

128 *The Scene of This World Is Changing*

(1 Corinthians 7:31)

To give us hope and to save us From sin and death that en-
The world a - round us is ail - ing. The wick - ed sys - tem is

slave us, His on - ly Son our God gave us— No
fail - ing. But God's rule we are now hail - ing; The

gift could have great - er worth.
King - dom has come to birth.

Chorus

Though the scene of this world is now

The Scene of This World Is Changing

(See also Ps. 115:15, 16; Rom. 5:15-17; 7:25; Rev. 12:5.)

129
Holding Fast to Our Hope
(Hebrews 6:18, 19)

Men have been grop - ing for cen - tu - ries in dark - ness.
"God's day is near!" rings the King - dom proc - la - ma - tion;

Vain is their quest as they try to catch the wind.
Men will no long - er cry out to God: "How long?"

Man's trag - ic flaw is re - vealed in its stark - ness:
Soon he will free all his groan - ing cre - a - tion.

None can they save, for they all have sinned.
Praise God Al - might - y, and join our song.

Holding Fast to Our Hope

Chorus

Sing with good cheer, for God's King-dom is here! His
Son's might-y reign brings us free-dom from fear.
Through him, at last, e-vil soon will be past; This
hope, like an an-chor, is hold-ing us fast.

(See also Hab. 1:2, 3; Ps. 27:14; Joel 2:1; Rom. 8:22.)

130 *The Miracle of Life*

(Psalm 36:9)

Ev-'ry new-born child, Ev-'ry drop of rain,
Oth-ers may give up, Lose their will to try,

Ev-'ry gold-en ray of sun, Each head of grain—
Ech-o-ing the wife of Job: "Curse God and die."

All are gifts from
We are not that

God; They re-veal his way.
way. Praise to God we give,

Mir - a - cles per-
Thank - ing him for

Chorus

formed by him sus-tain us each day. So, what are we to do with a
ev-'ry pre-cious mo-ment we live. So, what are we to do with a

The Miracle of Life

gift so rare But to love the One who gave it and show him we
gift so rare But to love the ones a-round us and show them we
care. No mat - ter what we do, We nev - er can
care.
earn it. This gift is still a gift— The
mir - a - cle of life. life.

(See also Job 2:9; Ps. 34:12; Eccl. 8:15; Matt. 22:37-40; Rom. 6:23.)

131 *Jehovah Provides Escape*

(2 Samuel 22:1-8)

The liv-ing God, Je-ho-vah, you have proved to be;
Though ropes of death en-cir-cle me, I call to you,
From heav-en you will thun-der and give forth your voice.

Your might-y works a-bound in earth and sky and
"Je-ho-vah, give me strength, and give me cour-age
Your en-e-mies will quake; your ser-vants will re-

sea. No ri-val god can e-qual what you have done—
too." From your own tem-ple dwell-ing, you hear my plea,
joice. You prove to be what-ev-er you need to be;

there is none. Our foes will be con-sumed.
"Shel-ter me; Res-cue me, O my God."
all will see How you pro-vide es-cape.

Chorus

Je-

Jehovah Provides Escape

ho-vah pro-vides es-cape for the loy-al. His ser-vants will
see what a might-y Crag is he. So with cour-age and
faith in our God, we spread the fame Of Je-
ho-vah, our Source of es-cape, and praise his name.

(See also Ps. 18:1, 2; 144:1, 2.)

132

A Victory Song

(Exodus 15:1)

Sing to Je - ho - vah. His great name is high - ly ex -
alt - ed. His proud E - gyp - tian foes, He has
cast in - to the sea. Praise Jah Al - might - y; Be -
sides him there can be no oth - er. Je - ho - vah is his

See now all na - tions Op - pos - ing the Sov - 'reign, Je -
ho - vah. Though might - i - er than Pha - raoh, They
too will suf - fer shame. Doom now a - waits them; They
will not sur - vive Ar - ma - ged - don. Soon ev - 'ry - one will

A Victory Song

Chorus

(See also Ps. 2:2, 9; 92:8; Mal. 3:6; Rev. 16:16.)

133 *Seek God for Your Deliverance*

(Zephaniah 2:3)

Na - tions a - lign as one, Op - pos - ing Je - ho - vah's
Peo - ple on earth now choose, Re - spond - ing to this good

Son. Their time of hu - man rul - er - ship By God's de - cree now is
news. We of - fer to all men the choice To hear or proud - ly re -

done. Rul - ers have had their day; God's King - dom is here to
fuse. Tri - als, al - though se - vere, Need not fill our hearts with

stay. Soon Christ will crush earth - ly en - e - mies. No
fear. Je - ho - vah cares for his loy - al ones; Our

Seek God for Your Deliverance

more will there be de - lay.
cries for help he will hear. Seek God for your de -

liv-er-ance, Yes, look to him with con-fi-dence. Seek his righ - teous-ness, Show your

faith - ful-ness, For his sov - 'reign-ty, take your stand. Then

see our God de - liv-er you By his might - y hand.

(See also 1 Sam. 2:9; Ps. 2:2, 3, 9; Prov. 2:8; Matt. 6:33.)

134 *See Yourself When All Is New*

(Revelation 21:1-5)

Just see your-self,   just see me too;   Just see us all   in a world that is
Now see your-self,   and see me too;   And look a-head   to a world that is

new.   Think how you'll feel,   how it will be,   To live in
new.   No sight we see,   no sound we hear   Will cause a-

peace, to be tru-ly free.   No e-vil one   will then pre-vail;   Rule by our
larm or give rise to fear.   All has come true,   just as he said;   Now o-ver

God can-not ev-er fail.   The time will have come for a
man-kind, his tent is spread.   He now shall a-wak-en those

See Yourself When All Is New

new earth-ly start, The song of our prais - es will pour out from our
sleep-ing in death; Their voic - es will join us with ev -'ry grate-ful

heart:
breath:
"Je-ho-vah our God, how well you have done! All things are

new by the rule of your Son. The full-ness of our heart o - ver -

flows in our song; All glo - ry and hon - or and praise to you be - long."

(See also Ps. 37:10, 11; Isa. 65:17; John 5:28; 2 Pet. 3:13.)

135 *Enduring to the End*

(Matthew 24:13)

God's Word and all it prom - is - es Give rea - son to en - dure.
Main - tain the love you had at first, Which some - how could be lost.
All those en - dur - ing to the end Are those who will be saved.

The things you've learned and come to love Are all well - found - ed and sure.
De - spite the tri - als you will meet, En - dure no mat - ter the cost.
The book of life will list their names, A rec - ord clear - ly en - graved.

Be sta - bi - lized in ho - ly faith, Keep - ing God's day close in mind.
What - ev - er test may come your way, Nev - er yield to doubt or fear.
So let en - dur - ance be your aim; Let it have its work com - plete.

Stand firm in your in - teg - ri - ty; By tests you will be re - fined.
Je - ho - vah will pro - vide es - cape, Our God ev - er will be near.
Je - ho - vah's fa - vor you will know; With joy you will be re - plete.

(See also Heb. 6:19; Jas. 1:4; 2 Pet. 3:12; Rev. 2:4.)